# Handbook of

# *Western*

## *Fly Fishing*

by

**Paul B. Downing**

MAJESTIC PRESS, INC.
P O BOX 1348
ESTES PARK, CO  80517
(970) 586–2411 — FAX (970) 586-0996

**Handbook of Western Fly Fishing**
©2001 by Paul B. Downing

**Published by**
*Majestic Press, Inc.*
*P O Box 1348*
*Estes Park, CO 80517*

**ISBN:** 0-9625311-6-2

**PHOTO CREDITS:** Photos by the author or unseen friends.

**Diagrams:** PERPETUAL CREATIONS
**Cover:** SYKES DESIGNS
**Printed by:** PATTERSON PRINTING

PICTURED ON THE FRONT COVER: Odessa Lake, a greenback cutthroat trout recovery site in Rocky Mountain National Park, Colorado. Cutbow (rainbow/cutthroat cross).

PICTURES ON THE BACK COVER: Author with rainbow at Lees Ferry, Arizona. Greenback cutthroat trout.

# *Dedication*

This book is dedicated to my father, Earle B. Downing, who taught me to fly fish, encouraged my intellectual curiosity, and shared his love of nature, and to my wife, Bobbi, who supports me wherever my interests turn and who taught me to enjoy the journey.

# Acknowledgments

I am deeply indebted to a large number of individuals, shop owners and guides who helped me learn about fly fishing in the west. I could not possibly acknowledge them all, although many are mentioned in the text. So, for those not mentioned below...thanks!

I had amazing support in my local area. Burn Sundell, now a guide in Ennis, Montana, was my first fishing partner and teacher in Colorado. The folks at the St. Vrain Fly Shop and the Estes Fly Shop were extraordinarily helpful, especially owner Dale Darling and manager Mark Rayman. The members of the Alpine Anglers Chapter of Trout Unlimited have been very helpful. Ron Hildebrand openly shared his techniques, flies, locations, and particularly his love of the sport and the country in which we practice it. I repaid him by catching his ear with a weighted nymph rig while floating Gray Reef. Hopefully my thanks here is better payment.

There are some who go far beyond the call of duty. Austin Condon and Brian McKinley have done that for me. I gave each a draft of this book and asked them to read it and tell me what was wrong. They both did, returning the manuscript with many helpful comments. With their input, the book is far better than it would have been.

Finally I wish to thank my wife, Bobbi for preparing the manuscript, providing editorial assistance, and support for the project. In addition, I wish to thank her for being willing to accompany me to spots all over the west where I fished while she simply enjoyed the scenery. Together we have explored some wonderful places.

# *Table of Contents*

*Fish on! Author on the Colorado River at Lees Ferry, Arizona.*

# Chapter 1

## The Magnificent West

### Why Western Fly Fishing?

I love being in this country. The sights, sounds and smells transform me into a simpler person. Applying intense concentration to fly fishing causes me to be more aware of the beauty and subtlety of Mother Earth. Western fly fishing is the unexpected. The mink scurrying over the rocks. The elk lifting his majestic rack to observe the quietly wading intruder. The dipper (water ouzel) flashing by then singing its heart out on a nearby log. The orange and vibrant red on the sides of a native cutthroat in the net. Gold sunsets and purple mountains. The smell of mint crushed beneath my feet as I sneak along a grassy bank. Breezes scented with spruce and pine. Hawks keening to their mates. Quiet places that give you the impression nobody has fished them for years yet are often only a few minutes from paved roads. Crystal clear streams that seem devoid of fish until your fly disappears. All these are part of the special experience that is western fly fishing.

I have been a fisher all my life. My father taught me to fly fish when I was young. The primary fishing near Milwaukee, where I grew up, was for bass and bluegills in small kettle lakes. My first fishing pole was a heavy bamboo fly rod. I can still remember those hand-size bluegills smacking my cork poppers and fighting their hearts out.

Over the years the fly rod gave way to spinning gear and Wisconsin lakes gave way to the Gulf of Mexico. I was an active fisher, but not a western fisher—certainly not a trout fly fisher. The only time I actively fly-fished for trout was on a meadow brook trout stream in Wisconsin while working for the Wisconsin Conservation Commission one summer during college many years ago.

This book evolved out of my personal need. My wife and I visited the mountain west on business several times in the early

1980s. We fell in love with the area and started planning our vacations there. Western fly fishing was inevitable.

When I arrived in the mountain west, determined to fish, I knew very little. I bought a starter outfit, some flies, and off I went. Success was, shall we say, meager. My only trout fishing experience was on that slow moving meadow stream. These western streams roared by. It seemed impossible that trout could live in this fast water. I didn't have a clue how to fish out here.

My first solution was to search for water more like the meadow streams I had fished on more than 20 years before. I found a couple and my success went up some. Still I would see fly fishers on those fast streams and hear about their success at the local fly shop. There had to be a way to learn how to fish this water.

The desire to learn how to fish this western water led me to books on the subject, but none of them seemed to apply directly to what I was seeing on the stream. They were too general, designed to be useful in eastern as well as western waters. I learned a bit, but was still fairly lost.

The breakthrough came when the owner of my local fly shop, Dale Darling of St. Vrain Angler (303–651–6061), convinced me to hire a guide. A half-day on the water with Bobby Zulig brought all that random knowledge acquired from books into focus. What he showed me wasn't in those books! There was a missing link. Finally all that stuff made sense. It was amazing (see Chapter 6 for this lesson). My fishing improved tremendously overnight.

Still there was lots more to learn. Pocket water, nymphing, structure, presentation, line control, rigs, flies. I learned over the years. The sources were many; books, magazine articles, guides, other fly fishers, and years of experience on the streams throughout the west. Yet I felt that I should have been able to find most of the basic knowledge I needed in one simple publication. The fact that I couldn't started me thinking about writing this handbook. I have grown to love western fly fishing and want others to experience this unique setting.

This book is designed to provide you with the knowledge you need to become successful fly fishing on western trout

*This yellowstone cutthroat from the Lamar River is typical of
the rewards from exploring western trout waters.*

waters. I have made it as simple and straightforward as possible.
One rod, two rigs, a few flies and techniques of how to present
them in the four main types of waters of the west are all that is
needed to get you from relatively lost to reasonably successful.

In any book there has to be a starting point. I assume you are
a reasonably competent fly caster—you don't have to be really
good…klutzy will do…in most cases casts are short. I also assume
that you know the required knots, understand about lines, leaders, and the different types of flies. Waders, wading boots, fly
floatant, nippers, weights, hemostat, net, etc. are equipment you
have used before. Beyond that you can be a novice to fly fishing or
an experienced eastern fly fisher. In either case, this book will help
you succeed on western streams. I'd like to believe it will help
western fly fishers as well.

Starting out with the above goal in mind, I became increasingly
aware that there was another important element in why I love
western fly fishing…discovering new places to fish! In every western state there are literally hundreds of places to fish for wild trout.
Roadside streams, high mountain lakes, big waters, little creeks,
the variety is amazing. Some waters are famous, some unknown.

I have had wonderful days on many of them. But the greatest joy is when I discover a new (to me) special piece of water. The hunt is as much a part of the enjoyment as the fishing success.

So in the second part of this book I offer you ways to find your own special places to fish. Information sources are extensive and varied. Books and magazine articles are a good starting point. Fly shops are a wealth of information. Don't forget the various state fisheries people. And in this modern day, the internet contains amazing new insights into where to fish.

I will tell you how I explore a new area and then list waters and sources by state. Armed with this information you will be ready to find your own special western fly fishing experience.

When you think of western fly fishing, you may envision wide open spaces, streams full of big trout, and complete solitude. That dream can be a reality but often at a price; sometimes money, sometimes a little hiking effort. The more famous streams can be crowded. On most days there are as many fly fishers on the Bighorn in Montana as there are on any eastern stream. On other streams a crowd would be one fisher every mile or so. A crowd can be avoided and better fishing reached by a short hike. A half-hour walk can often get you all the solitude you wish.

Fish are not all big. My average is 10– to 12–inches. Sixteen–inchers are good fish most places and largest of the season in others. Fish over 20–inches are considered trophy fish everywhere, even though virtually nobody keeps a trophy any longer, thank goodness.

While there are some circumstances where the wild trout could be classed as inexperienced or even dumb, most fish are smart and wary. Clear water and abundant predators keep trout on edge. There are as many trout out west with a Ph.D. in fly fishers as there are in the east. Don't expect easy pickings. I have had many 50–fish days. Thirty–fish days are not uncommon but I still get skunked several times each year.

Western fly fishing is beauty and challenge combined, making the total experience special. That's what it's all about. Western fly fishing is a great joy. Come join me in the journey.

*Richard Osmond admires the beauty of western trout country on the way to Frying Pan Lakes in Colorado.*

# Chapter 2

## Fish Remembered

One of the great joys of having fly-fished the west is the memories I have gathered. Special fish and special places that, when recalled, live again. Some fish were special because of their behavior. Exotic locations accounted for several fond recollections, but just as often I remember fish from easily accessible, even highly popular locations. So, the following are some special fish I remember. I hope that by telling these stories I give you a better impression of what fly fishing in the west is like.

### Risers

One day in October I fished the Big Horn in Montana with guide Roger Rehurek of Cottonwood Camp (406–666–2391) and his Old English Sheepdog Harley. Roger said there was a midmorning spinner fall he hoped we could catch. Catch it we did. As we floated down the river there were several back water areas where a trout or two were rising to a No. 16 Parachute Adams.

At one point Roger pulled the boat to shore and we piled out. Harley went off investigating "dog stuff" as we approached a large stand of cottonwoods overhanging the edge of the river. There, stacked up along the shore, were at least six trout rising to spinners. They were nicely spaced a half cast upstream of one another. Some right on shore, some out a bit.

I tried the nearest one. A take on the first cast. Harley suddenly reappeared, barking and carrying on, helping as best he could to land that fish. A nice 16–inch brown was released quickly... without canine assistance.

Others were still rising, so I tried the next one upstream. After a couple of casts I got the fish's feeding rhythm just right and had another fine brown on. At this point Harley decided he'd better hang around or he would miss something. Stepping up two feet I repeated the act with the third nice brown.

That fish was a lot tougher. I floated that fly over it numerous times. He kept on feeding, often taking a natural not a foot from my fly. Finally I struck at what I thought was a take but it turned out he had taken a nearby natural. That spooked my fish but not the others. They were still actively rising.

The next fish was up and slightly to the left, so I didn't have to move. Again timing the feeding pattern just right and getting the fly in the fish's feeding lane produced a take. Another nice, fat brown came to hand, this one pushing 18–inches.

I thought surely this fish had spooked the last feeder but no, it was still actively rising an inch outside a weed patch. Just as I was about to move to cast to him, my problem child began to rise again. Well, what the heck, let's give him one more try. I couldn't believe it, he came up for my first cast. I don't know what was different, but I definitely enjoyed my success.

That left one last fish, the one rising an inch from the weeds. Naturals would pass two or three inches out and be ignored, but let one get next to the weeds and it was gone. I didn't want to hook the weeds, which would spook it for sure. My casts would land too far out. Again and again my fly would be ignored as it drifted two or more inches from the weeds. Once I got one close but the fish had just taken a natural and was down. I kept casting, determined to get everything just right. Finally I did. The fly drifted right next to the weeds, almost touching them. A head rose majestically, its mouth opening to engulf the fly. What a sight. An honest 18–incher, rich browns and golds in its pre-spawn dress.

Incredible, I had caught every one of the risers in that pod. Six beautiful browns from 16– to 18–inches. I don't know who was happier . . . me, Roger, or Harley.

## *Trout and Mink*

The Provo in Utah is one of my favorite places to fish but it can be quite crowded. One day a fly fisher was in each of my favorite spots so I went looking for new territory. Downstream from where I usually fish is Bridal Veil Falls, a spectacular and justly famous tourist attraction. It plunges hundreds of feet from a cliff into the Provo. I decided to try fishing a few hundred yards upstream. This part of the Provo is below a major diversion dam so the flow was much reduced. The current wandered between large boulders and into deep pockets, a challenge to wade. Scrambling over the boulders, fishing the pockets, I was rewarded with an occasional 12–inch trout.

The one I especially remember was no more spectacular than the others. It was just that I almost missed him. You see, I was distracted by a rustling on the far bank. There, not thirty feet away, was a mink looking at me as if to say I had no business invading its territory. A moment of eye contact and it was off, its rich brown fur glistening in the sunlight filtered by its personal tree. Staring and remembering its presence, I was distracted again. This time it was the insistent tug of a trout on my line.

## Firsts

Ever since I can remember, I have wanted to travel to Alaska and fish for salmon. Streams in the wilderness full of salmon packed shoulder-to-shoulder from one bank to the other created a lure I finally could not resist. Lots of research and many phone calls yielded the name of Paul Allred, Ouzel Expeditions (800–825–8196). Paul flies groups into the headwaters of the Salmon River (and other rivers as well) where they float downstream and fish for a week. Just what I wanted, a true Alaskan wilderness adventure.

It started out just as I had expected. A small plane ferried groups of four people into the wilderness, nothing but bogs and mountains to be seen in any direction. We landed in an impossibly small clearing in the pines, the prop almost touching the first tree as the plane stopped. Whew, we made it!

The next couple of hours were spent carrying gear and food for the week to the stream, inflating and packing the rafts. A short float brought us to our first overnight, a sandy beach next to a large pool After setting up camp, it was time to fish!

I asked Paul what he would suggest. "The grayling are thick in the pool," he said. "Try a Black Gnat." So I did. I was immediately into 14– to 18–inch grayling, lots of them, my first ever. They came at that fly from every angle. Some even leapt out of the water and took it on re-entry. These wonderful iridescent blue-on-gray marvels were as enthusiastic as they were beautiful.

Finally, they stopped taking a dead drift. I made a mistake tightening my line, causing the flies to drag across the surface. Wham, another grayling! The drag brought them up almost every cast. Finally it was time for a food break.

After a late dinner it was 9:30, but in early July Alaska's sun had not begun to set so it was back to more grayling. As I was entertaining more fish, Richard Mickelson, one of the other clients, discovered a school of king salmon further up in this big pool. These are the largest of Alaska's salmon, some running to near 100 pounds. The average on this stream was 30– to 40– pounds...a lot of fish in these small headwaters.

Richard hooked one on a fuchsia Woolly Bugger. After a fierce battle the fish broke loose, but not before I had a good look at him. Forty pounds of salmon on someone else's fly rod was too much to bear. Forget the grayling...I was now a salmon fisher.

Tying on a Beadhead Black Woolly Bugger I drifted it to the pod of salmon. After several drifts the line tightened and just as quickly went slack. No fly. Whatever took it was big! I decided to try that unlikely fuchsia Woolly Bugger. You can see that fly for a mile even three feet down. On one drift I saw a large female move slightly to the left and open her mouth. My fly disappeared and I set hard. This was a huge fish and my first salmon on a fly. She bolted downstream, then back up and then down again. I was helpless to stop her. Finally she settled into a bulldog fight at the bottom of the pool above a long, very shallow riffle, well into my backing.

As I hurried downstream to gain line and angle, Paul asked about my equipment. I was using my 7–weight Scott rod and the 10–pound tippet I had forgotten to change in my excitement. He informed me that combination would never hold a king.

The salmon was beginning to tire though and I had to work with the tackle in my hand. As I made my way downstream, she made another upstream run. Deciding this was the wrong course of action, she headed for the sea over 1000 miles away. In between was that shallow riffle. She floundered and fell on her side. Rick Neubauer, another fly fisher in our group, set out to net her while I tried to untangle the line she had lodged under a boulder. Rick reached her just as I got my line free. He was already reviving her as I ran up. I admired the exhausted salmon briefly, measured her at 49 inches with the marks on my rod (probably the largest I will ever catch) and lovingly released her with a belly full of eggs to go back to her final job.

Paul said that large females like that run about one pound per inch. I would never have landed her had she not floundered on the rocks and Rick not been on the spot with a net. Luck, fate, clean living; call it what you will. In any case she was beautiful, huge and free to reproduce more of her kind. Perhaps some day I will return to catch her children or grandchildren. For now, even though it was still light enough to fish, it was almost midnight. I was beat. I headed to my tent, happy to end a perfect first day.

## Ghost Pool

One day I was fishing a private water section of the Arkansas River above Salida, Colorado when I had a most unusual experience. It was pre-runoff spring, a point in April when the water is low, clear and warming, but runoff from the mountain snow melt had not started.

As I worked my way upstream, I noticed a big boulder sunken in the middle of the river, its head just above water. The current swept to either side of it and rejoined 20 feet downstream. A shelf on the left created a riffle just above the boulder which broke into a deep hole. As I approached from below, the water was so clear that I was up to my thighs in water that appeared to be inches deep. I could see every pebble in that hole. It looked to be only 3– to 4–feet deep, but I was already in 2 feet of water that was getting deeper fast.

Even though I could not see any fish, I decided to give it a try. Setting up my rig with a weight and two flies, a No. 16 Flash Pheasant Tail and a No. 18 Beadhead Brassie 8 feet below the strike indicator, I cast into the pool. As the rig swept up the tailout the indicator hesitated. "It must be a rock," I thought, because I could not see any fish where the fly was, or anywhere else for that matter. On instinct I set the hook and was surprised to feel a fish on the other end.

What was it? I didn't have a clue. I had a ghost on the line. I peered into the water. Even in the clearest water imaginable, with less than 20 feet of line out, I could not see a thing. No movement, no flash of a side, just an apparition moving my line along the bottom. Finally I raised the apparition to the surface. It was not until it was within netting distance and on the surface that the ghost dissolved into a fat 13–inch brown.

It was amazing how well this brown blended into its background. A great help to its survival I am sure, but browns are native to Europe, not Colorado. How could I not see that fish resting in this clear water or even on my line? It was a spooky experience, but one I repeated as I took several browns from that pool, each ghost no more visible than the first.

## *Backyard Greenbacks*

Lily Lake is a small pond on the edge of Rocky Mountain National Park just 15 minutes from my office. My friend, Burn Sundell, convinced me we needed to take a long lunch and give it a try. What can I say. When it comes to fishing I'm an easy sell, so we were off.

We started fishing along the shore. Nothing much was happening but I was not sorry I came. The pond is one of the most beautiful locations in the world. It is nestled among the mountains, its shore covered in wildflowers and pine trees. To the south, Long's Peak looms 14,255 feet high, its snow-covered peak reflecting on the surface of the pond. Songbirds and ducks fill the air with their bright music.

Burn had gone ahead of me and broke my reverie by waving me to the top end of the pond. There, at what passed for an inlet, the surface was alive with rising trout. They were taking something just below the surface. Burn and I tried various nymphs. Finally Burn hit on it, a No. 16 Flash Pheasant Tail with no weight. We would cast it out and retrieve it with almost imperceptible movement. Suddenly the line would tighten and we were onto another fish.

What fish. The males were spectacular. Green backs meld into vibrant vermillion sides and an orangish belly. Large spots increase in number toward the tail. The females are equally spectacular. Their sides are a reddish-orange. Both have the characteristic red slash-like marks on their lower jaw that distinguish them as cutthroat trout. At that time I knew nothing about them. I just knew they were beautiful and hungry. We caught a number of 12– to 14–inchers before they quit and we went back to work. I ate lunch at my desk, entirely lost in the beauty of that lake setting and the trout living there.

Later I learned a great deal more about these greenback cut-throat trout. They are the official state fish of Colorado and the

**Lily Lake Greenback**

only native trout of the front range of the Rocky Mountains in Colorado. Once thought extinct, they have been reintroduced into a small portion of their native waters in Rocky Mountain National Park and elsewhere on the front range. Successful re-introductions have allowed the greenback to be downlisted from endangered to threatened. They are one of nineteen or more native cutthroat subspecies found throughout the west. Some populations are in good shape but most are threatened or en-dangered due to over harvesting in the 1800s and competition from exotic trout...rainbows, browns and brook trout...that have been introduced to their native waters.

There is something extra special about fishing for these wild native trout in their native habitat.

## Lunchtime Rainbow

In my continuing exploration of places to fish in the west, I came upon an ad for fly fishing in south central Utah. It prom-ised excellent fishing for browns and rainbows in the Fremont River. I called John Campbell of the Outdoor Source (435–836–2372) to make arrangements. He booked me into The Lodge at

Red River Ranch. The Lodge is a delightful place with comfortable rooms and an intriguing three story log great room. The Fremont is just down a path into the pasture. The river winds through the valley against a red rock bluff. Classic western scenery. After settling into my room one May afternoon, I went out to explore the river. I had some success that afternoon but the best was yet to come.

The next morning John met me at The Lodge and we fished the river. In this area the river consists of bend after bend with 10–foot high banks and deep pools. We stripped Woolly Buggers through these pools to be occasionally interrupted by a feisty brown trout.

At lunchtime we sat on a gravel bar at the inside of a bend pool. The high bank across from us sported several small bushes which overhung the water. As we talked of fishing and times past, we noticed fish rising under the bushes. Closer observation disclosed several different fish. One was a large rainbow who came up deliberately to sip small mayflies. Watching her for 20 minutes as we finished lunch was fascinating. She lived in a dark little area not a foot off the high bank. She would rise up, gently take her next snack, and slowly sink down out of view. Finally, it was too much. Lunch was interrupted.

The cast was tricky. I had to thread the No. 16 Parachute Adams between two overhanging bushes to land it as close to shore as possible. The first cast landed short. I let it drift downstream a bit so I didn't spook the rainbow. As I was about to lift and recast, a 12–inch brown splatted the fly. Fortunately my rainbow was still rising.

Drying the fly, I cast again. The fly made it through the opening and landed close to shore, just as I hoped it would. As the Parachute Adams floated down to her, the rainbow rose deliberately, looked at my fly and refused it, her nose not an inch away. I thought I had her. Several more good casts brought no interest whatsoever, but she was still rising to naturals.

In these circumstances I have learned to go to the next smaller fly, so I tied on a No. 18. Another good cast. She rose, opened her mouth and took the fly gingerly. I lifted the rod to feel a slight resistance, then nothing. I missed her. This time I had spooked her for sure. She quit rising. So it was back to our interrupted lunch.

As John and I finished desert (Carolyn Campbell's delicious cookies), we noticed that the rainbow was rising again. Savoring my last cookie, I decided to give her one more try.

Same cast, same drift. This time she came up and took the fly more confidently. I had her...if I could keep her out of the brush, that is. It all worked out. John netted her, a 16–inch beauty with the vibrant red stripe so characteristic of wild rainbows. After releasing her carefully, we celebrated by sitting back down, sipping a soda and reliving the scenery and events of the past half-hour. Truly she was a fish I will always remember.

## The Path to Glory

Sometimes you have to roll with the punches. Some friends and I had planned a trip to the Green River at Flaming Gorge in Utah one June anticipating great cicada terrestrial fishing. We arrived to learn that the water release from the dam had been increased to 8500 cfs...flood stage. High but still fishable we were told. No cicadas though.

We parked at Little Hole and walked upstream along the newly improved path. In several places the water covered the path to a foot or two. As we turned one corner we noticed a strange thing. There were two good fish on the path. Skitterish, they took off the moment we saw them. Over the next couple of days we caught a lot of fish at the edge of the normal streambed where the high water covered the bank outside the path. Clearly the fish were trying to keep out of the heavy current. We continued to notice fish on the path in several places, but fly fishers were passing frequently, scaring them. There were plenty of other fish to catch, but catching one of these skittish fish on the path became a challenge to me. I would cast to a fish only to have it run for the cover of deeper water.

The last day I got up a little early. I had a plan...get to the path before any fly fishers had scared the fish! Perhaps then I could get one to take my fly.

I arrived to a totally empty parking lot. Not a fisher in sight. So far, so good. Just upstream from the parking lot was the first place where the path was flooded. On the shore side it was lined with cattails. On the river side a little strip of drowned grass separated the path from the river. The water over the path was about 18 inches deep and fairly slow.

Approaching from downstream I looked for a fish. At what would be the head of a pool were it not a path, I spotted one. At this point the water from the river broke over a low point in the bank and flooded the path. Just below the break, settled where the water calmed, was a fish. I set up to cast into the faster water of the break where I hoped my fly would drift down to this fish without scaring it. As they say, the best laid plans! The fly

*Brown caught on the hiking path, Green River, Utah*

landed in the faster water and stopped. I had hooked the flooded grass. Surely I would spook this fish as I pulled the fly free.

As I lifted my rod gently to free the fly, a strange thing happened. It started to move. Another fish, lying invisibly under the rougher current of the break in the bank, had taken my offering. The trout headed through the break and into the safety of the river.

Just what I wanted. Now I didn't have to contend with all the snags on the path. Typical of a brown, she bulldogged it deep, shaking and twisting. Tiring she allowed me to net her at the edge of the flooded grass that had been home a few minutes before. I released this chunky 19–inch brown with thanks and a great sense of accomplishment. I had caught a trout on the hiking path of the Green River. How many others could make that claim?

## *The Winner*

First light revealed the rich purple-red that made the Vermillion Cliffs famous. As I drove toward the boat landing, shear monoliths towered over me. The black night sky turned slightly blue in the east and stars winked out, lost in the brighter light of dawn. It was early January and I was going to fish my traditional first of the year location, Lees Ferry on the Colorado River in Arizona. What could be better? Fly fishing for chunky rainbows in one of the most spectacular canyons in the world while the streams up north are covered with anchor ice and blanketed in snow.

I met my guide, Bob from Lees Ferry Anglers (800–962–9755), at the dock. This is not a place you can get into without a boat. I didn't have one. A guide with a boat and great local knowledge was the perfect solution. We headed upstream as the sun just kissed the western rim of the canyon. Any day on this river canyon is special, but this one offered a fish to remember.

After fishing several locations with mixed success, we made our way to the island below the dam. Bob had seen several fish feeding there a couple of days before. We landed the boat and waded out onto a gravel bar. A shallow channel cut the bar in two. There in the channel were several actively feeding rainbows. The main source of food for these fish were tiny midge emergers. My 5–weight was rigged for deep nymphing but Bob's 4–weight had two midge emergers with no weight, so he had me use his.

I positioned myself to cast so the flies would drift naturally through the channel. As I did, I noticed that one fish was much bigger than the others. With Bob looking over my shoulder…both of us excited about this fish…I made my cast. After several drifts the fish were still actively feeding, just not on my flies. One would raise or lower slightly and their mouth would open and close quickly on a tiny, invisible bug. How these big fish thrive on such small insects has always amazed me.

Finally the large fish rose slightly; moved to the left and opened its mouth just as I thought my flies passed her. Lifting the rod, I felt the weight of a big fish. She felt the resistance of my pressure. The fight was on.

Downstream she ran, gone for sure if she didn't stop. Back upstream, trying to hide in the channel. Still facing resistance, she bolted to the surface and jumped just feet in front of us.

A monster…the biggest I had seen in this water. We marveled at her as she jumped again, then headed back downstream. Again she turned and came back. As I got her closer she noticed Bob's net. Wanting nothing of that, she bolted for the nearest cover, the back of the boat, hanging out in the current. Under she went.

Bob told me to keep the line away from the bottom of the boat as it was rough and the line would be cut. Not good news. I had a large, uncontrollable rainbow on a 4–weight and 5X tippet. She could go wherever she wanted…and did.

Getting the rod as low as possible, I coaxed her out from under the boat. Home free, I thought. But it was not to be. She saw the net again and thought the boat looked better. Seconds later the line went slack, cut on the rough edge of the boat.

She had defeated me. A trout with a tiny brain had outsmarted a reasonably intelligent human. Good for her. May she prosper and spawn many like her. She was probably the biggest rainbow I have ever hooked (Bob estimated her at 26– to 27–inches) but that's okay. I hooked her, fought her, and got to admire her spirit as well as her beauty. I didn't mind losing her, I was going to release her anyway. Still, I would like to know exactly how long she was. A picture would have been nice too.

## *Western Memories*

These are only a few of the memorable experiences I have had in my pursuit of western trout over years past. I invite you to join me in this most special experience as I explain how I catch fish in western waters and explore how you can find your own "special place."

# CATCH-AND-RELEASE

**M**any popular western streams are not fully protected by catch-and-release regulations. They are at risk of serious population declines caused by keeping fish. Pressure from those who wish to keep fish ...not all of them bait fishers as is popularly assumed...make changing this situation politically difficult. Some states prefer to stock trout and allow capture instead of controlling the take from a wild population. While this situation is slow to change, there is hope for these populations. A large percentage of western fly fishers practice catch-and-release on all waters. Many outfitters require it of their clients as do owners of private waters. One set of statistics show that over 30 percent of the rainbows, browns, and brook trout caught in Rocky Mountain National Park were kept in 1985. Today fewer than 5 percent are kept.

**T**o preserve the wild trout populations in western streams, I suggest that you adopt catch-and-release. That practice will help preserve the wild trout populations that have provided me with such wonderful memories, allowing them to provide you with some as well.

# Chapter 3

# *Seasons of the Trout*

Western fly fishers do not think of seasons in the ordinary way. Rather, the seasons revolve around water and fishing conditions. Seasons run from pre-runoff to runoff, to normal summer to low water, fall to winter. These seasons can be further subdivided by prominent hatches. So seasons may be known as the early blue-wing olive (BWO) season, the caddis season, the green drake season, the hopper season, or the late BWO season.

One of the beauties of western fly fishing is that the seasons come to different elevations at different times. Spring ice-out can be as late as July in some high mountain lakes. Lower lakes and streams may be past runoff and into prime summer hatches by then. Fall comes early in the high country so the whole season is compressed. This variation in seasons gives the fly fisher the luxury of deciding what kind of fishing is preferred and seeking out the locations which have the proper conditions for that type of fishing.

## *Pre-runoff*

The sun is warming the stream and most of the ice has melted from the shore. Water is low. Trout, emerging from a sparse winter, have increasing metabolisms and a voracious appetite.

This is the season of the early BWO hatch. These little mayflies are present in most western streams. They do not hatch every day, seeming to prefer dark overcast to bright sun. In these early spring days, the hatch, if there is one, will be in the warmest part of the day. It is often sparse, but some days it can be exceptionally thick.

I recall one day when a light, gentle snow sprinkled the frosty 40 degree air. BWO duns were everywhere and trout were up after them. A No. 18 BWO color Parachute took fish after fish for over two hours. Then the clouds thinned, the snow stopped and the sun cast a faint shadow. The hatch was done and so was the fishing. Western fly fishers will seek out these drab snowy days hoping for just such a hatch.

Even without a hatch, pre-runoff is highly productive. The trout remember their last BWO feast and regularly see BWO nymphs. Since the water is low and light is more subdued, this is a great time to use a dry and dropper. I start with a No. 16 BWO Parachute on 5X. For a dropper I will use a No. 20 Flash Pheasant Tail, a No. 18 Beadhead Pheasant Tail, or a No. 18 Beadhead Brassie. Most fish will take the dropper. If there is no activity on the dry, switch to a No. 12 Coachman Trude or a No. 16 Elk Hair Caddis. (See Chapter 4 for this rig and Chapter 5 for my list of universally effective flies.)

Fish the seams in the slower runs or in pocket water. This cool water keeps the trout's energy low so they usually stay out of the faster water. Look for fairly shallow water with direct sun as this warms up some and is more comfortable for the fish. Also, the warmer water has more active bug life.

As the weather warms, the BWO hatch gives way to a caddis hatch. This hatch can be truly spectacular. The caddis hatch on the Arkansas River above and below Salida, Colorado...known as The Mother's Day Hatch...is justly famous. The town even has a weekend festival in its honor. This can be your best chance all year to catch a large brown or rainbow on a dry at mid-day. There are many other western streams with important caddis hatches during the pre-runoff season. Finding your own private caddis festival or unknown BWO hatch is a special treat.

## Runoff

As the sun warms the mountains, the snow melts and the streams fill with runoff. The melting progresses up the mountains. The result is a month to two month long period of high water in lower elevations. Streams in the high country have shorter runoff periods.

High, fast and often off-color water puts fly fishers off. Surely this is tough fishing, they think. To some extent that is true. However, some great fishing is available in swollen streams.

The secret is to reason out where the fish are. They will be looking for slower water. This water can be found in pools, behind rocks, and especially along the shore. I described fishing on the edge in Chapter 9. This is a great season for those techniques.

In one stream I fish regularly this time of year, I have found a number of unlikely hiding places. High water runs through the shoreline willows. Occasionally there is an open pocket in or at the downstream edge of a willow stand. When this pocket slows the water and there is easy access to the main current for escape, trout will congregate. A well-placed fly will take them. The willows serve as a current break and bug attractor. Fish this slower water like pocket water. I like to use a No. 16 Beadhead Prince or a No. 16 Beadhead Brassie as a dropper with a No. 12 Coachman Trude as the dry. The bead makes the fly more visible in off-color water. The red of the Coachman attracts the fish. I seldom have to use anything else.

Be careful in this fast runoff water. The bottom is less steady with the fast water so rocks move at the worst possible time. The current is often stronger than it looks. Take no chances. I never wade more than calf deep under these conditions.

The runoff season is also a great time for ponds. I always get in a couple of trips to my favorite ponds this time of year. I love the signs of spring; geese on nests, red-winged blackbirds in the cattails, spring flowers. As a bonus, the fish are active all day and often near the surface.

Runoff also gets me thinking about tailwaters. Often water is retained in the reservoir for summer release so water levels downstream of the dam are relatively low. The dam ensures that the water is fairly clear, even if it is high from releases. Bug activity is high due to the warming of the sun. This is a great time for nymphing with No. 16 Flash Pheasant Tails and No. 20 Western Midge Emergers. (See Chapter 5.)

## Summer's "Normal" Water

As the snow is almost gone from the high country, the streams retreat back into their banks. Conditions return to normal; or what fly fishers think of as normal. Many anglers only fish during vacations taken in July and August when the streams are fairly full and fast but not wild. In fact, this condition is only normal for that brief period. Still it is the standard we use to compare water levels.

The summer's normal water coincides with periodic mayfly, stonefly and caddis hatches. These vary by stream so check locally. However, in the absence of specific information and not observing a hatch, there is a safe bet for most any western stream. Trout will take flies that look like mayfly and caddis nymphs. Often they will come up to dries that look like the adults. My starting combination on a new stream under normal flow is a No. 12 or No. 16 Coachman Trude or a No. 16 Parachute Adams with a No. 18 Beadhead Brassie.

Fish pocket water, seams in the riffles, breaks in the runs, and shoreline structure. Watch for terrestrials, especially later in the summer season. Hoppers and ants can be deadly. By the way, a No. 12 Coachman Trude does a credible job of passing for a hopper if you don't happen to have hopper patterns along.

This is the season when time of day takes on importance. Baring a mid-day hatch, trout are more active in the cooler low light of morning and evening. A mid-day hatch may not even bring the fish up, but they will often take dries in low light even without a hatch. Still, midday can be good fishing. It is just that the trout are more likely to be feeding on nymphs near the bottom in deeper water.

## *Falling Water*

As summer evolves into fall, the snow melt is done and water slowly drops. This is the time of gin-clear runs that appear to be only inches deep. It is also the time when rainbows and cuts start feeding voraciously in preparation for winter. Brown and brooks prepare to spawn. Bug activity is high. The fish are shallow and active. It is my favorite time of year. Crisp days and cool nights move the hatches more toward the middle of the day. The lower sun makes it more likely that fish will feed on the surface.

The dropping water concentrates the fish. They can be found in impossibly shallow and unbelievably clear water. Phantom fish appear from nowhere to attack your fly.

Rainbows and cuts are found anywhere there is a break in the current. Hatches are tending back to the midges and small BWO of pre-runoff. It is a great time for No. 18 Beadhead Brassies and No. 18 Parachute BWO.

Browns are gathering on the gravel flats thinking about spawning. This is the time when the big browns come out of the deep holes. It is a great time to strip streamers and Woolly Buggers.

Fall bugs are smaller than those of summer, so get out the No. 20's or smaller. Terrestrials are often still active, but again smaller. Downsize your tippet along with your flies. 6X is standard in this clear, shallow water (except for streamer stripping, of course).

Variety is the watchword. There can be several types of bugs available. Fortunately, these actively feeding fish are not often fussy. Anything that looks like food usually works. It is rare that you will need to fish the bottom with nymphs. Most of the fish are in the shallows and looking up. By the way, when you encounter a hatch of two different bugs, studies have shown that the trout will be feeding on both but will key in on the larger one. Try this. Put on an imitation of the largest dry then add a smaller dry as a dropper. This two-dry rig can really work.

Perhaps it is the beautiful falls colors. Or the smell of dried leaves and wood fires. Or the honk of geese heading south that make this a special time. In any case it is a time not to be missed. In the west it can be enjoyed longer. Fall comes early in the high country and progresses down into the valleys. I follow it whenever I can.

## *Winter*

At some point fall fishing moves into winter fishing. Unlike the slow transition from summer into fall, the arrival of winter fishing is sudden. A cold front will come through and linger for longer than normal. Snow will spit. Even after the air warms again and the sun is out, something is different.

The trout are no longer in the shallows. They have moved to the deep runs and pools. Bugs may still be on the surface but the trout probably aren't.

Fish can be caught, but they are far fewer than just the week before. Time to dig out the nymphing rig. Bounce flies off the bottom. It is time again for midge emergers.

In some waters trout season closes for the winter. In others fishing is permitted all year. However, as the streams ice up and the ponds freeze over, most fly fishers retire to the tying bench to reminisce about the past season and dream of fish to come. Others don't give up.

*Early winter snow brings on a blue-winged olive hatch.*

Where to fish in the winter? Many streams will have sections which remain clear over winter. On a warm day, dress accordingly and give it a try. Western fly fishers look forward to days with a gentle wet snow and no wind. This is the time when blue-wing olives will hatch near midday, a rare chance to fish drys in the winter. Even a couple of trout will make it feel like spring. Just be careful of the ice.

Better yet, find a tailwater where the water released from the dam is warm and the stream is clear of ice. Tailwaters such as the Big Horn in Montana, the Miracle Mile on the North Platte in Wyoming, the Frying Pan and Blue in Colorado, Lees Ferry on the Colorado in Arizona, the San Juan in New Mexico are each famous for their cold weather fishing for big trout. Almost all streams are dammed, and below those dams some open water will be found, especially if they are bottom release dams. Search around and talk to other fly fishers. You will have some winter tailwater fishing available somewhere.

The other alternative is to go to one of those famous tailwaters. They are great fun and already quite popular. Dress warm. There is nothing worse than standing in a stream with toes so stiff you can't safely wade, or arms shaking with the first signs of hypothermia. This can be avoided with a trip to your local fly shop or outdoor store. Loose fitting thermal layering is great. Thermal *and* wool socks in boots big enough to keep circulation going are required. When you start to chill, take a break. Warm up by going inside or moving around. Play it safe and the rewards can be great.

The sky is leaden. The air calm. Snow is spitting. The geese are flying so low you can hear the air whistle off their wings. Trout are occasionally interrupting the drift of your nymphs. What a great experience. Don't expect to be warm. Don't expect 50-fish days. Just remember that the alternative is sitting at the tying bench dreaming.

The seasons of the trout each has its own special character. I look forward to them all.

# Guidelines for Releasing a Fish Unharmed

1. Play and land a fish quickly. The ultra-light rods that are in vogue can seriously reduce the survival rate of released fish if their use results in a prolonged fight. Use a net with a catch-and-release netting on larger fish. This controls the fish more easily, allowing for quick removal of the fly.

2. Keep the fish in the water while removing the hook. When touching the fish, use wet hands to reduce damage to the protective slime on the fish's skin. Do not squeeze the fish.

3. Handle the fish as little as possible. Remove the hook gently. Barbless hooks, or hooks with the barbs pinched down, make fly removal quick and less damaging. Barbless hooks have no appreciable effect on the number of fish landed. Often purposely releasing the tension on the line when the fish is close enough to land will allow it to slip a de-barbed hook, thus eliminating the time and trauma of handling the fish. If a fish has swallowed the hook, or has it caught in a gill, do not try to remove it. Instead cut the line. The hook will work loose shortly.

4. Release the fish into quiet water. Revive it so that it is breathing normally and swims off on its own.

# Part I

# Equipment, Flies and Techniques for Western Waters

The following chapters present my way of fishing western waters. It comprises a set of equipment, flies, and techniques that I have learned, developed and modified over the years. Using this system you will be able to catch fish under almost any circumstances. They are not the only way—perhaps not even the best way—but they have worked for me in many different waters.

*Success comes from a simple rig.*

29

*Chuck Rizuto lands a rainbow at the San Juna
River, New Mexico.*

# Chapter 4

## Rigging for Success

When I first started getting serious about fly fishing for trout, I read books and articles on the subject. The suggestions as to flies, rods, reels, and line were as varied as the authors. Under some specific circumstances each would work well. However, I wanted something different. I wanted a setup that would work all the time as conditions changed on a stream and as I moved from big stream to small stream, to lake or pond. After substantial experimentation, I have developed my basic rig. A rod, reel and line that always work...will almost always work... two methods of presenting flies which cover almost all western streams, and a set of flies that will catch trout most of the time. This is a lot to claim, especially given the huge variety of gear and flies recommended by others. Indulge me. I believe you will find that my system works.

### Rod, Reel and Line

#### Rod

Fly rods come in many weights and within each weight different types of bending action (fast to slow.) I have found that one weight is almost universal in its application. It is not always the best choice, but it works.

I recommend a 5–weight rod. The choice of fast or slow action...or something in between...is up to you. Test alternatives out at your local fly shop. Remember that in western streams you will almost never cast over 40 feet and frequently casts are 10 feet, so select a rod that works well for you on that length of cast. A rod that works well on long casts, but not on short ones, will prove to be a problem for you. If you have a 4–weight or a 6–weight, don't go out and buy a 5–weight. You can do well with what you have. Remember you can be a klutzy caster and still catch fish. Find what works well for you...not what the salesperson thinks is the best rod going.

Why a 5–weight? It is refined enough to present a small midge without too much disturbance, yet strong enough to move a strike indicator with some weight through a stiff wind—a frequent occurrence on western streams. A 2– or 3–weight will present the midge better but cannot handle the heavier rigs. A 7– or 8–weight does not do well with the midge but is better than the 5–weight for heavy nymph rigs and streamers. Still, the 5–weight is the best compromise.

There is an advantage to the one rod approach. Instead of spending a modest amount on each of three different outfits, you can spend a little more on a better 5–weight outfit and save the money you would have spent on the other two. It will be cheaper in the long run.

I can hear you now. "But Paul," you say, "what rods do you have?" I admit that I have five, a 3–weight, two 5–weights, a 7–weight, and a 10–weight. The 3–weight I use on small streams near home during low water and in the high country on hiking trips. I usually don't take it on trips. The 7–weight was purchased for salmon in Alaska. I use it occasionally on western streams under extreme conditions when the wind is heavy and so are the flies or when it is streamer time. The 10–weight is for king salmon and salt water. It never gets used on western trout streams, but does see some bass and northern action. If you find me on a stream, I will almost always have my 5–weight.

The rod should be 8½– to 9– feet long. A shorter rod allows easier casts among bushes but requires a longer reach in close casting situations. Since most western streams are relatively open, the longer rod is the better compromise.

### Reel

In western streams a reel must do two things, hold line and provide modest consistent drag when fighting a large fish. Fortunately, there are many reels in the low to intermediate price range which perform these two functions well. You do not need to spend a fortune on a reel. I love my Ross Gunnison reel. It is smooth due to the ball bearing arbor and the drag is delicate.

Once you get your reel, set the drag quite light. You can always add more drag with your hand if you need to. More fish are lost at the end of a long run by a drag set too tight. The small diameter of the remaining line on the arbor and the resistance of the water on all that line between you and the fish increase the drag. A drag that is not too light at casting distance may be too tight just when you need it most. Err on the light side. Recently there has been a big push toward large arbor reels. They reduce the gain in drag that results as line comes off the reel. They could save that big one for you.

## Line

Since most of your casts will be relatively short, you need a line that puts enough bend in your rod to cast effectively at short distances. You need a weight forward floating line. A floating line is essential to most of the fishing you will do and can be made to sink in those rare occasions when it is needed. Marry it to a 7½ foot leader tapered to 4X. You will add tippet to this.

## Knots

I am not a big fan of fancy knots. I never seem to remember how to tie them without a book in front of me. People have argued that I need these fancy knots because they are stronger than the old simple ones. When a knot is tied in leader material the knot will break before the leader material, thus prematurely releasing your fish...usually that really big one. The loss in strength can be 30 percent or more, depending on the knot.

While I continued to use my simple knots, I felt a bit guilty. Fortunately Bernie Taylor got me off the hook. In an article called "Testing Knots" (*Fly Fisherman,* Dec, 1995, p.52) he showed the loss in strength from various knots. Amazingly, my simple old knots fared well.

To tie the tippet material to the leader, I use a triple surgeon's knot. It was rated as the strongest of the knots he tested. To tie the tippet to the fly I use the improved clinch knot. This one was the worst of the knots he tested but only by a small amount. It was only 14 percent weaker than the best knot, which is really complicated to tie. The best simple knot, the Orvis knot, was not much stronger than the improved clinch. My conclusion; stick to my simple knots. I do have a fly break off every once in awhile, but it is rare and usually attributable to an overzealous set.

To attach the leader to the fly line, I use either a loop or a nail knot. There is good and bad about each and I still seek a better alternative.

The loop is a woven mesh design with a loop toward the leader end that slides over the end of the fly line and is secured by a piece of plastic that is melted onto the line. The loop allows me to change leaders or add a sinking tip quickly. However, it tends to sink. This sometimes causes drag on a fly just when I don't want it.

The nail knot takes longer when a change in leader is required. Alternatively, a section of leader material can be tied to the fly line with a nail knot and a loop can be tied in the other end. Then a sinking tip or a new leader can be added loop-to-loop. The nail knot prevents most of the sinking of the end of the fly line. Unfortunately it makes another problem I have with both methods worse.

Every method of attaching the leader to the fly line leaves a knot or some other added bulk to the end of the line. When fighting a fish, if the line is pulled in so that this bulk passes through the tip eye of the rod, it will often hang up. This is not so bad when pulling line in, but is a real problem when the fish decides to take off again. A hang-up then could cause a lost fish as the line breaks or the hook pulls out. Of all the systems I have tried, the loop causes the least problem. The nail knot can be a lot worse if the butt material of the leader is thick. The leader, attached by a nail knot with a loop tied into it, has two knots to hang up so it is more of a problem. What would be ideal would be a totally seamless, flexible connection. I have not found anything even approaching it yet.

## Rigging

I have found through experimentation and experience with guides throughout the west that there are two basic rigs which will allow you to present your fly correctly and hence catch fish in most circumstances. Both are two-fly rigs. One is the dry fly and dropper. The other is the double nymph. While these rigs may not always be the best for a particular situation, one or the other will work in almost every case. When they don't, the alternatives are just variations on these basic rigs.

## The Dry and Dropper

This is simplicity itself. Add about 2 feet of 5X tippet to your 4X leader using a triple surgeon's loop. Now tie on a No. 12 attractor dry fly or a No. 16 Parachute Adams with an improved clinch knot. Tie 1½– to 2 feet of 5X or 6X tippet to the bend of the hook. Now tie a small size 16 to 20 nymph or emerger fly to the other end (treat the dry but not the nymph with floatant) and you are ready to fish.

This combination is an excellent rig for exploring new water or determining what the trout are feeding on. I use it 70 percent of the time that I fish western waters. The dry fly acts to attract the fish and as a strike indicator. It allows you to see if your flies are floating naturally (good) or dragging (usually bad except when that trout you least expect nails it!) If it disappears without a splash, something, hopefully a fish, is on the underwater fly. Under most circumstances a large percentage of the fish (75 percent or more) will take the underwater fly. In fact, trout feed underwater far more than on top. I love to catch trout on dry flies. But when they are not up, which is most of the time, I can watch the dry as if I were dry fly fishing and have just as much fun with the take.

We will talk about your choice of flies in the next chapter, but let me lay out two basics here. The dry fly must be large enough that the underwater fly does not continually drag it under. And it must be easily visible in rough foamy water. If you cannot see the dry, you will miss takes on the underwater fly.

That's all there is to the dry and dropper rig. It is the most effective combination I have found for fishing the shallow water of smaller streams or the edges of the larger streams. Try it, you will love it!

## Double Nymph

This rig is basically the same as the dry and dropper except for the addition of a strike indicator and weight. Tie 2 feet of 5X tippet to your 4X leader. Tie on a nymph or emerger. Tie another 2 feet of 5X tippet to the bend of the fly using an improved clinch knot. Guides differ in their opinion as to whether to tie this second tippet to the eye of the fly or the bend of the hook. Each claims that the upper fly drifts more naturally if tied as they suggest. I have found no obvious difference, but usually tie mine to the bend because this is what I learned first. Now tie your second underwater fly to the end of the second tippet, again with a clinch knot.

The next step is to add weight. I use one split-shot just above the knot between the 4X and 5X. Split-shot tends to slide down the line in use, so the knot prevents slippage. Also, the shot is not likely to weaken the 4X to below 5X strength when pinching it on unless you use too much pressure. Please use reusable tin shot, not lead. Lead is poisonous to fish, birds and the insects they feed on. We have enough problems with water quality without this added burden.

Opinions vary as to whether to use one larger shot or several smaller ones. Fishers argue that several small shot allow the line to drift more naturally. I find they are more inclined to tangle. With reusable shot I can easily remove my weight and replace it with a larger or small one. I only use two shot on those rare occasions when one large shot is not enough weight.

Strike indicators are many and varied. Paste on tabs, removable putty, and small bobbers are available but the cheapest and simplest to use is yarn. I use synthetic macrame yarn available at most hobby stores. A hank...enough to last several lifetimes...costs a couple of dollars. Color? Choose a color which will be easy for you to see against a white, blue, and brown background. Select a medium tone, not real light or real dark. You want the indicator to blend in to the sky when the fish looks up but still be visible to you.

Attach the yarn indicator as follows. Cut off a piece of yarn about 1½ inches long. Separate the individual strands (usually 6 in macrame yarn) and use two or three of them. Make a circular loop in your leader near the fly line, the thick end of the tapered leader. The lower line should be in front of the upper line. Then pass the lower end of the leader partway through the loop from the back to make a second loop. Tighten the first loop enough to remove slack, leaving the second loop sticking through it. Don't make it snug. The line should still slip though this tightened loop when pulled from the bottom, the end of the leader where the fly is attached. Now place the yarn through the second loop, center it and tighten by pulling the lower part of the leader. The second loop will try to pass through the first, but the yarn will stop it. Get it good and tight. Then fluff up the yarn and add dry fly floatant. To remove the indicator later, simply push the line up from the lower leader and the second loop will open (unless the yarn is tangled). Alternatively, pull one end of the yarn through the loop. Remove the yarn and pull both ends of the leader to remove both loops. Your leader will be slightly kinked, but this causes no harm. Use as small an amount of yarn as will keep your indicator afloat and be visible in rough water. Most fly fishers use way too large a clump of yarn. Large wads of indicator yarn make it difficult to cast the rig and could spook fish. They are also less sensitive in indicating subtle takes.

The distance between the strike indicator and the weight is determined by the depth of the water to be fished. The general rule of thumb is that this length should be approximately 1½ times the depth fished. This is because the indicator on the surface will float faster than the weight near or bumping the bottom. Thus the line will be upstream of the indicator and extending at an angle. The angle, and thus the length needed between the indicator and the weight, depends upon the speed of the water (faster water means more angle) and the weight (more weight means less angle). I find that if I use the 1½ rule and adjust the weight so that it bumps the bottom occasionally, it puts my flies where they need to be.

If you need more leader to get down to the bottom, add more 4X between the leader and your 5X tippet. A total length between the strike indicator and the fly of more than 10 feet becomes difficult to manage to get a natural drift (unless in a drift boat) and perhaps more important makes it almost impossible to get a fish close enough to net. Fortunately these extra long leaders are required only on rare occasions.

This nymph rig is cumbersome to cast until you get used to it. To learn to handle it, cast more slowly and wait longer on the backcast pause. Watching the line over your shoulder will help get the timing right. I tend to use more arm and let my rod reach further back to compensate for the weight and the air resistance of the indicator. Stick with it, you will learn quickly enough.

The nymph rig is most effective in the deeper and especially faster water characteristic of many large western streams. It is most effective when fishing the main currents of these waters.

Some friends whom I highly respect argue that two-fly rigs should not be used because they cause a lot of foul hooking which can damage trout. It is true that I foul hook a fish occasionally. The most frequent occurrence is when a trout hits the dry and I do not hook it solidly. As the trout fights, the line sometimes wraps around its body. Should the dry fly come loose, the dropper fly can foul hook the fish, usually in a fin. Similarly, a trout taking the upper fly on a nymph rig can wrap the line around itself and become foul hooked on the lower fly.

For me, foul hooking is usually a rare, but still bothersome, occurrence. When I start having problems with fish being lightly hooked on the dry, I change the dry to a smaller size. This will frequently solve the problem by not allowing the fish to slip the dry fly hook.

If you have a consistent foul hooking problem with the two-fly rig, try different size flies and/or different lengths of line between the flies. If the problem persists, switch to a one-fly rig. Instead of a dry, use a small piece of indicator yarn. You will not get the dry hits, but the indicator will tell you if your dropper is floating naturally.

We are now ready to go fishing...except for the flies.

# Chapter 5

## *Flies*

When discussing fly fishing with others, I get the impression that most fly fishers think that the fly is the most important part of trout fishing. Observe fly fishers on a popular stream. One catches a fish. Another yells over "What are you using?" for the successful fisher must have found *the single fly* that will take trout that day!

Some days that is true. I recall one afternoon on my local stream when there was a blue-wing olive (BWO) hatch (a small green-bodied mayfly.) Trout were taking surface flies everywhere. My standard fly for this hatch...which had worked at this very spot many times before...is a No. 16 Parachute in BWO colors. With confidence I tied one on and got...well, I got ignored! It was maddening. I changed to a smaller size. Still nothing. Then I found a different fly in my box with the hackle at the front and little gray wings. As this fly touched the water a nice 12–inch rainbow took it. I caught several fish on this fly in exactly the spots I could not get anything on the parachute alternative. In this situation, an active rise to a specific insect, the exact fly can make a difference as it did this day. But on most days a fly that is generally the right shape, size and color will work just as well.

Notice that the successful fisher is not asked how the fly was presented. Was it on a drag–free drift? Did you twitch the line? How much weight did you use? What length of leader? What weight of tippet? What kind of water did you find the trout in? No, it is just "what fly" they ask! Yet I have found that presentation—how a fly is presented and where in the stream it is fished and how it moves through the water—is far more important than the specific fly used. Still the fly is necessary and fun to talk about and sometimes makes or breaks the day.

I have purchased or tied hundreds of different flies over the past several years. I have fished these flies in all different situations at different times of the year and in many different streams. The result is that I have come up with a small set of simple flies that work under a wide variety of situations. This basic selection is what I offer here. Most of these flies are available in fly shops or can be tied easily. With them you will succeed in catching fish in western streams. You can add to this basic selection from local fly shops when special conditions require it.

## *Dry Flies*

Dry flies are intended to imitate actual bugs on the surface or to attract fish to the surface even though they do not look like natural food.

Attractor flies are intended to grab the attention of a trout that is not actively rising to a surface fly but is willing to avail itself of an easy meal when the opportunity arises. Hence they are not intended necessarily to imitate any particular natural fly, although some do.

The Stimulator is the most popular attractor pattern, followed by the Parachute Grasshopper and the Royal Wulff. However, I find none of these universally effective. Instead my basic attractor fly is the **Coachman Trude** on a No. 12 or No. 16 dry fly hook. I tie the wing with clear white Antron yarn and make it extra bushy for added floating and visibility. Add a little yellow calf tail above the white wing to make it more visible. It is amazing how well this pattern works in a wide variety of situations. It is the one I tie on first when I am at a new stream with no visible hatch.

In most western streams, there are frequent but sparse hatches of caddis flies and various mayflies. These are usually small flies. Thus I have developed a generic attractor fly that simultaneously imitates each type of fly, at least close enough to attract trout who are accustomed to seeing the natural flies on a regular basis. I call it the **CMA** (Caddis Mayfly Attractor.)

The CMA is easy to tie, but you won't find it in fly shops (yet.) Start with a standard No. 16 dry fly hook (I use Tremco 100). First I tie in several hackle fibers for a short tail. Then dub a body of Antron. Next tie in a trude wing of white Antron and clip it short (about to the bend of the shank.) I try to make it flare to the sides. Finally tie in a sparse hackle and finish the head. I tie it in gray, green, brown, cream and yellow, each with the appropriate hackle color. If I see any flies around the stream

I am fishing, I use the CMA in the appropriate color for my attractor. If you do not tie yourself, a good substitute for the CMA is the standard Elk Hair Caddis. You should have some of these for the occasional caddis hatch anyway. To add visibility, try overlaying yellow calf tail as an upper wing.

The third fly pattern I use as attractor is the standard **Parachute Adams** in various colors as listed for the CMA. I use a light gray post to make it visible and sometimes trout key in to it more readily than the CMA or the Coachman Trude. You will need this fly for mayfly hatches anyway, so stock up. I use No. 16s most often but I am finding that No. 20s work better under some circumstances. You must use a small dropper fly like a No. 20 midge emerger with a No. 20 parachute attractor to prevent the dropper from sinking the small attractor.

These three patterns work as well as any in the typical western stream situation where there is not an active hatch. In most active hatches the parachute works well so other dry flies are not necessary except on rare occasions.

## *Dropper Flies*

The dropper fly I start with when fishing a new stream or a stream I have not fished for a while is the **Beadhead Brassie** tied on a No. 16 nymph hook. Frequently I never change. It catches fish. I am not sure exactly what the trout think it is. It doesn't look like a midge or a red worm. It is perhaps closest to a caddis nymph or perhaps a mayfly nymph. But who cares? It works in a wide range of situations. I think the extra weight of the copper wire gets it down to the fish better. I have tried versions of this fly which use hackle or CDC (cul de canard) instead of or in addition to peacock herl. They work better in a few cases but not as well in most, so I have settled on the standard pattern as my basic dropper fly. The two other universal dropper flies I use are the **Flash Pheasant Tail** tied on a No. 16 or No. 20 nymph hook and a **Beadhead Prince Nymph** tied on a No. 16 hook.

I admit to one other dropper fly, the **egg** (or glow bug.) During spawning seasons it is especially effective as trout feed on the escaped eggs of spawners. Some fly fishers feel that this fly is inappropriate and should not be used. It seems to me, however, that it imitates a natural food source just like an insect-based fly or a worm-based fly does.

Finally, under some circumstances like a tailwater where I know the trout feed a lot on midges, I will use a midge emerger as my dropper fly. I will describe my generic midge emerger in the midge section of this chapter.

These are my go to dropper flies. You will seldom need anything else.

## Nymphs

My standard nymphing combination is a No. 12– or No. 16– weighted Beadhead Prince Nymph and a No. 20 midge emerger. I make three varieties of the Beadhead Prince Nymph. One has a brass beadhead and no weight on a No. 16 nymph hook. This is for shallow water nymphing. My weighted  version has the brass head and 7 wraps of lead on the shank of a No. 12 nymph hook so that it will sink fast. I have not been able to find a satisfactory alternative to the lead yet, but I am looking. The third version, which is part of what I call my rock series, uses the lead body and the extra heavy titanium beadhead on a No. 12 nymph hook. This I use for deep or fast water situations. An even heavier rock series uses two titanium beads and lead on a No. 10 long shank hook. Believe me, it gets down. On a recent trip I used the rock series Beadhead Prince along with an egg and a BB shot on a 10–foot leader and a floating line. It reached the fish on an 8–foot deep gravel bar. I was rewarded with two nice cutthroats.

The other flies I use as the top fly for the nymph rig are the Beadhead Pheasant Tail or sometimes an egg. However, the prince works well in most situations.

## Midge Emerger

The most common fly I use as the bottom or dropper fly in a nymphing rig is an emerging midge. I have adapted a generic emerger pattern to make my own simple **Western Midge Emerger**. Using a standard No. 18 nymph hook I produce the body simply by wrapping the shank with tying thread of the desired color. No tail. I have tried a tail and it works just as well, but no better, so why bother. Sometimes I will dub the body with the desired color of Antron instead. I wrap the body moderately thin and build up a hump about one-quarter of the way back from the eye. Then a ribbing of fine gold wire is added to the body to segment it. I tie a sparse shock of light gray Antron in front of the hump like a trude wing but very short to simulate the wing case and finish off the head. With the hump the Antron spreads to the sides. I clip it quite short so that one-half the body extends beyond the Antron. Simple, but very effective.

Midges are non-biting bugs that are similar to mosquitos. Their larva are thin and have a thickening of the body at the top third. When preparing to hatch, the shuck comes off at about this point. The Antron simulates this situation.

*Big fish can be caught on small flies*

I do not tie this, or any other fly, very neatly. Frequently there will be errant strands of Antron sticking forward or down from the head. I just clip these off close to the body leaving little stubs. I think this roughness makes the fly look more natural but perhaps I am just using this as an excuse for inexpert fly tying. The most effective colors for this **Western Midge Emerger** are black, chocolate brown, gray and olive green.

Other flies I use as droppers on a nymph rig are the No. 20 Flash Pheasant Tail, the egg, and sometimes the Beadhead Brassie.

## *Midges*

Probably my most frustrating time when fishing western streams is when trout are taking midges on the surface or just below it. I have fished and fished and been ignored by every trout within a mile on numerous occasions. But I am getting better. Part of the secret in this case is the fly.

The standard dry fly for midge hatches is the No. 20 **Griffith's Gnat**. I have had success with them on occasions when clusters of spent midges are floating on the surface. I especially like a Griffith's Gnat with a white Antron post I ran across at the Flaming Gorge Lodge Fly Shop at the Green River in Utah. It is more visible so I can detect strikes more easily.

I also tie a small generic **Midge Dry** that Mark Rayman of the St. Vrain Angler Fly Shop in Longmont, Colorado showed me. Using a No. 24 dry fly hook dub a sparse body of the appropriate color and tie in hackle at the head. I had a hard time finding small enough hackle until Mark told me that he just clips off the extra length after he has finished the fly. It works great. That's it! No wing. No tail. Combined with a midge emerger, I started having much better success in these difficult hatches. But I am still looking for a better fly for when trout are taking midges on the surface.

Recently another fly fisher showed me a **CDC Midge Emerger**. Simplicity itself, consisting of a lightly dubbed body and a CDC wing case. It has to be fished without floatant because the oil makes the CDC clump together. Fished dry, it has been very successful on some occasions but less successful on others. The jury is still out but it currently appears to be better than the generic midge dry above. (See Chapter 12.)

## *Woolly Bugger*

Easily the most universally successful streamer fly is the **Woolly Bugger**. It works as an attractor fly when stripped or dead-drifted through runs or pools in streams, but I have found it most successful in ponds and lakes. It is the first fly I go to in these waters.

The most effective colors are a matter of opinion. Olive and black are most commonly used. In Alaska a variant called the egg sucking leach is used. This fly has a long shank (3X) and the head is a yarn egg or glow bug. The most common color is purple but fuchsia is also very effective. This fly is effective in the west as well as Alaska.

At a fly shop in Basalt, Colorado, I ran into a black Woolly Bugger with a body made of peacock cactus chenille. The tail was black as was the hackle. In place after place I have found that this variant works better than any other black and usually better than any other color. In Alaska a purple or fuchsia egg sucking leach with the appropriate cactus chenille has proven more effective at times. I have both plain chenille and cactus chenille in all colors but I always try the cactus variant first.

## *Egg*

The yarn egg is a very effective pattern when spawning fish are present. Trout feed on escaped eggs. In salmon streams they lay below the redds to intercept loose salmon eggs. In all western streams they do the same. Even if there are no redds in the immediate area, trout key into the egg. It is a natural food like the nymph. I see no moral difference. Others differ in their opinion so add it to your box or not as you see fit.

Well, there you have it, the basic set of flies—twelve in all—I use in western streams. I am sure someone will be shocked that I did not include the special fly they have great success with. But my basic flies work. If you fish them with proper presentation and the confidence you place on your special fly, you probably will not need that special fly or the "hot fly" the local fly shop or catalog is pushing. If you are like me, however, you will have to buy that hot fly anyway. It may just be the ticket and in a few cases it is, but mostly it is not any better than this set of basic flies. I have a large stock of other "special" flies I seldom use. Still, some day, like that BWO hatch we talked about, a "special" fly will be the only thing that works and I will surely be glad I had it. Besides, buying the local "hot fly" supports the fly shop that just told you where to go to get fish. Also, it may end up being added to "your" basic list as I have recently added the Post Griffith's Gnat to mine.

*Large fish love Woolly Buggers.*

# Chapter 6

## Pocket Water

As you will recall, if you read Chapter 1, I came to fly fishing for trout in the Rocky Mountain west from a background of bass and bluegills in Wisconsin. Prior to moving to Colorado, my trout fishing had been restricted to one farm meadow brook trout stream. These roaring mountain streams out west were a bit much for me. It seemed to me they were running way too fast to hold trout. Yet others at the local fly shop recounted success after success in these waters. They called them "pocket waters." I purchased the recommended flies and tried. I even caught an occasional fish. But I wasn't comfortable with this kind of fishing. Instead I sought out slower meadow streams that were more like that stream in Wisconsin. I met with some success but I kept hearing about excellent fishing in the faster waters. I had to learn about this type of fishing!

### Learning Pocket Water Fishing

One early spring day I was talking to Dale Darling, owner of the St. Vrain Fly Shop in Longmont, Colorado (303–651–6061) about my problem. He made the best suggestion I had received on the issue. He suggested I hire a guide to teach me how to fish this pocket water. He recommended a half-day wade trip with Bobby Zulig, a young guide working out of the shop, who loved to teach people how to fish. At first I resisted the idea. Real fly fishermen (gender intended) do not hire a guide! Guides were for inexperienced non-locals who didn't know any better. But then it hit me. I *was* an inexperienced non-local who didn't know much. Dale guaranteed that the trip would be the best money I had ever spent on fly fishing. So I gave in and signed up for the next afternoon.

I met Bobby at the shop and off we went. He stopped at one of the swiftest parts of the stream, a section I had seen several fly fishers on in the past but which looked impossibly fast to me; especially under the current high water conditions. We put on our waders in a cool May breeze, but the glowing sun warmed us.

The first surprise, Bobby tied a dry fly (No. 12 Royal Wulff) on my line and then a No. 16 Beadhead Pheasant Tail on a dropper. I had never heard of a dry and dropper rig before. Bobby explained the dual functions of the dry as indicator and attractor. It made instant sense. (See Chapter 4 for instructions on this rig.)

As he prepared my rig, he explained about the type of water we would be looking for. Trout need three things: food, comfort and safety. Trout live in slow areas (seams) in the water which are near deeper water or boulders for safety. These seams have actively running water but not too fast for comfort, and are in areas that channel food down to them. These areas of slower water are called pockets and it is in these pockets that trout sit and feed. This simple explanation made sense.

We then walked to the stream and studied it. We moved beside a large boulder in the middle of the stream with its head above the water. Bobby pointed out how the stream flow piled up against the front of the boulder before it split. It then swept past the sides of the boulder and came together at full force further downstream.

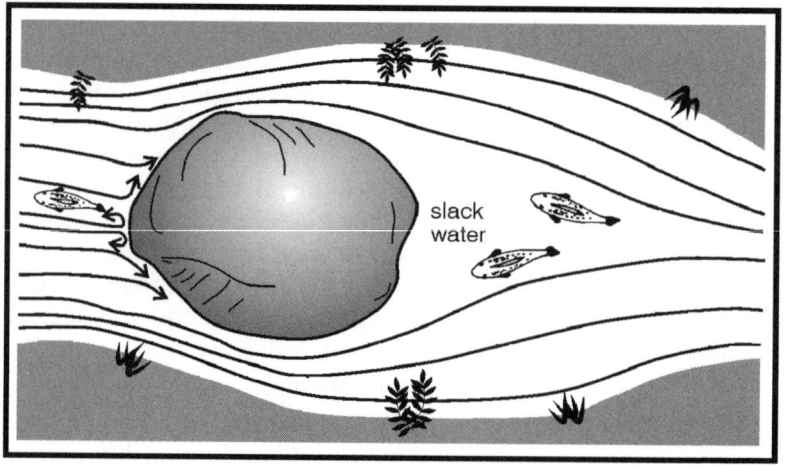

*Figure 6–1*
*Pocket water holding areas*

The result was quiet water directly behind the boulder which gradually gained speed as it joined the diverted current downstream. This is the pocket. It is small and shallow (1– to 3–feet deep) with slow current right next to fast water. My skepticism that it held fish continued. (See Figure 6–1.)

Bobby explained that the ideal home for a trout was just where this slow water started to pick up speed as it joined the diverted faster water. It is called the seam. This location provides food as the fast flow meets the slower flow and suspended food drops from the current. It provides comfort as the trout do not have to work as hard to keep in feeding position, and it provides protection as the trout can move under the boulder when threatened. He also pointed out how the feeding lane can often be spotted by the location and speed of bubbles on the surface. These bubble lines are an indicator of the location of the pocket. You fish on the slow-water edge of these bubbles.

I was then ready to fish. However, casting from beside the boulder where we stood would be a disaster. The flies would be quickly dragged out of the slower current behind the boulder by the fast water currents going around it. I needed a slower drag-free drift if the trout were to take my flies.

Bobby moved us directly downstream from the boulder and slowly moved up to what I thought at the time was an impossibly short casting distance. Surely we had spooked any trout in that pocket.

Bobby then told me to strip off about a rod length of fly line. I now had a total length of line of 9 feet of leader and 9 feet of line beyond the tip of my rod. I was to cast to the seam between the faster and slower current toward the back edge of the boulder. When I did, almost no line hit the water, only leader. A total distance of about 20 feet away the flies landed from my extended rod with a slight plop. Bobby then told me to lift my rod as the fly drifted back to keep the line off the water and remove slack. He also told me to watch the dry fly closely for any movement and to set the hook at the slightest twitch of the fly.

Once I learned to cast this short line accurately and raise my rod at the right speed to prevent drag or slack—a slow learning process met with consummate patience by Bobby—it was amazing how natural a drift could be achieved. The difference in location of the cast made a huge difference in the drift. A few inches to the right and the fly would be in the swift water racing downstream far faster than trout would wish to chase it. A few inches to the left and it would almost stop dead in the water directly behind the boulder. The seam between the two contained water at the speed preferred by the trout. As I practiced accuracy and line control, I learned how the current acted behind that boulder. That drifting dry fly confirmed everything Bobby had explained. I also learned a bit about what the faster and slower water looked like. The bubbles were not the only clue. Careful observation revealed where the slow waters were and where disturbed waters and fast currents existed.

Another thing happened as I practiced behind that big boulder. A trout took my dropper fly and my dry fly danced and dipped under the water. Bobby announced "fish" and I set the hook...too late and too hard and with too much slack. All I got for my effort was a splash as the trout waved goodby with its tail.

This is not bass fishing. You do not have to force a hook through a bony jaw. I had to learn that a light-but-quick tightening of the line accomplished by a raising of the rod is sufficient to hook a trout in such a short-line situation. Still, that trout gave me confidence that what I was learning would work.

After we had covered an area behind the boulder with several casts, we would move up. One step or so only. Then we covered the new area. After several steps we covered the entire area behind the boulder. We moved on to another pocket.

Bobby would point out a pocket. I would approach it carefully from downstream, positioning myself to make these impossibly short casts. I had to select a position where my line would not cross any of the faster water. A drag-free drift could be accomplished only if the line and leader were in the slow water of the pocket or in the air above the fast water. With practice I got better. Bobby no longer needed to point out when and why I had drag. After a while I could present a fly without drag most of the time. I would cast to each pocket five or six times. If there was no strike Bobby would say "Nobody home," and we would move up.

Over the next two hours we slowly covered no more than 200 yards of stream. In that time I acquired the basics of pocket water fishing, hooked and released a few trout, missed several more, caught bushes and a prize fly-eating tree (a close relative to Charlie Brown's kite-eating tree), and fumed at my incompetence and slowness to learn.

Still, I learned more in that half day than I had taught myself over the past two years. Dale was right. It was the best money and time I could have spent, thanks to Bobby.

## *Types of Pockets*

Pockets of slower water in a rapidly moving stream are found in several locations, not just behind boulders that stick up above the water. Any place the swift current is slowed by an obstruction can create a pocket.

Take that boulder for example. A boulder on the surface will often create that nice trout-holding pocket I have described. In addition, it may produce a pocket in front of the boulder. When the full force of the current reaches the boulder the current has

***Typical pocket water.***

momentum. It tries to plow through the rock. When it can't, it often piles up against the face (upstream) of the boulder before it slips to the sides around it. Over the years it may erode a deep hole in front of the boulder as the current continues to hit it. This piled up water forms a pocket of slow water near the bottom and just in front of the boulder. Trout (one or more) will live in this type of pocket, dashing out into the current for food. Cast above the boulder and let the top fly slow in the bulge in front of the boulder. The dropper fly will be down in the pocket until the dry is sucked to the side by the fast water. There are often sticks caught in the bottom here so expect to loose a few flies.

Pay particular attention to pockets where the runout of one pocket, that is where the current just starts increasing in speed, runs into another boulder. The soft water in front of the second boulder will almost certainly contain a trout.

Big boulders will sometimes create another pocket just at the downstream edges of the exposed rock. The current swirls into a small back eddy. Sometimes when conditions are right, it will hold trout. They are just where the back eddy rejoins the main current around the boulder. This may be close to the boulder or it may be a little bit downstream. Cast to the downstream flowing water just above where the backwater enters to get a natural drift through this water.

Don't neglect submerged boulders. They create the same slack water pockets. It's just that there is an additional, faster current *above* the slow water. This makes it more difficult to present a fly correctly, but it is not impossible to catch trout from such pockets.

Try to present the dropper fly so that it just misses or even touches the top of the boulder. The current that passes over the top of the boulder will expand into the space behind it, slow and drop some. If you present your fly just right and are lucky, the fly will follow the back of the boulder down into that slower water where a trout is waiting.

It is more difficult to get this presentation right. Try to get the dry fly indicator somewhat upstream of the dropper fly as it passes over the boulder. Also, make sure there is enough line between the two flies to allow the dropper to reach into the pocket behind the submerged boulder. It will take practice and experimentation, but in the end it will be rewarding. I have caught some of my largest fish from these submerged pockets.

Another favorite pocket of mine is just above a small waterfall or plunge pool. The current piles up as it meets the barrier that causes the fall and a pocket of slow water is formed. A fly cast above the fall will slow a bit just before it tumbles over the edge. Often enough a trout smacks it just as it slows. They don't have much time to make a decision so the take is hard. They also frequently miss. But it is great fun.

This is a difficult spot in which to get a drag-free drift. The plunging water is faster than that above it. It will drag the line and fly as it breaks over the edge. This requires very short casts and a very high rod to keep as much line off the water as possible.

Don't neglect the plunge pool itself. There is another slower water pocket just downstream from where the falling water hits the lower surface. Rainbows will often live here. They will chase flies as they drift from the plunge to the tailout where the current speeds up. This may only be a couple of feet, but be sure to fish the drift out into the faster water as strikes often come just as the fly starts to accelerate.

I cannot tell you all the good pocket water spots. You must learn from your own experience. Pay attention to where fish are found and where they are not. But don't expect hard and fast rules. Some pockets that simply scream "fish" never have a trout in them and others that look less promising are productive. The best idea is to cover all the pockets as if they hold trout. You will be surprised how many actually do.

If you are fishing in streams with different types of trout, play attention to the various speeds of water moving in the pockets. Fast pockets will hold mostly rainbows. Slower pockets will hold browns and cutthroats. Those backwaters at the edge of large boulders are loved by browns. Rainbows love the area just above a boulder or plunge pool and the plunge pool itself.

Once you learn how to effectively fish pocket water you have an excellent chance of success on most western streams. Not all streams or all parts of any single stream will be pocket water. But you will learn to look for the seams between faster and slower water that trout feed in. You will then place your fly where the trout are most likely to be feeding and present it in a drag-free drift. The reward for learning pocket water fishing will be more success on all types of water. An extra bonus is that most fly fishers avoid pocket water so even on crowded streams you may have it all to yourself. I have never used a guide on pocket water since that first day, but I am sure glad I did it just that one time.

# Chapter 7

# *Nymphing*

The sky was leaden with an occasional snowflake drifting by. Canadian geese flew so low overhead I could almost feel the air move over their wings. I cast my nymph rig upstream, put in a big upstream mend and played out line as the strike indicator drifted downstream on the current. The indicator hesitated briefly as the flies ticked a submerged boulder. Then the indicator disappeared. Gathering up my slack I set the hook. No worry about getting this fish on the reel! He went downstream in a flash and took out half my backing. Then he jumped and, thankfully, headed back upstream in the heavy current. Ten minutes of give-and-take brought him to my net. A beautiful 25-inch male, the identical brother to the one I had caught behind that same boulder a half hour earlier, gleamed as I removed a No. 20 Flash Pheasant Tail from his lip and set him free. This was great nymphing. I reflected on the fact that three days before I didn't have a clue about how to do it!

Like pocket water fishing, I learned basic nymphing from a guide. I had heard and read about the outstanding fishing at the tailwaters of Navajo Dam on the San Juan River in New Mexico. Consequently, I made plans to go down in mid-February to try it out for a few days. The people on the phone at Abe's Fly Shop (505–632–2194) told me it was mostly nymph fishing. I had never been nymph fishing before and wasn't even sure if I knew what that meant except, of course, one would use nymph-type flies some distance under the surface. Well, I had learned my lesson with pocket water fishing. I confessed to the person on the phone that I had never been nymph fishing and would need a guide to teach me—stressing the word *teach*. I arranged for a one day wade trip. Again, it was some of the wisest money I have ever spent in fly fishing.

## *Basic Nymphing*

I met my guide, Mike Sulkowsky, at the shop and off we went. As we headed toward the catch- and-release water just below the dam I explained my need to learn. Mike promised to teach me what I needed to know and to get me into some nice fish in the process. He delivered on both promises.

We waded across a shallow flat to a swift run. Like the pocket water back home, it looked impossibly fast. Surely no trout would be in that water. I expressed my doubts. Mike explained that the current was fast at the surface but at the bottom it was slowed by the resistance of the rocks and boulders. The trout lay in this slower water near the bottom waiting for food to come by.

Mike suggested I use my 5–weight rod equipped with floating line. To this he added a strike indicator, a weight, and two impossibly small flies. (See Chapter 4 for this rig.) He carefully explained how to tie on the indicator. I then expressed my doubts about catching the big trout the San Juan is noted for on such small flies. Mike explained that tiny midges and worms are the main diet of these tailwater trout. Bigger flies just do not work most of the time because the trout never see large insects so do not think of large flies as food. To prove the point he turned over a rock to expose hundreds of these tiny insects and worms. There was nothing under that rock bigger than a No. 20 hook.

## Mending the Line

Once rigged, Mike led me out into the current about knee deep. He told me to cast three-quarters upstream and allow the line to drift drag free in the current. After several casts I started to get the feel of this heavy rig. I made a fairly decent cast, allowed the line to drift, and almost immediately saw the strike indicator drag across the current. Mike told me to "mend the line." I didn't have a clue.

The idea is to allow the flies and indicator to drift along at the same speed as the current. This dead-drift presents the flies the same way naturals would drift, thus fooling the trout. Frequently the water between you and the indicator is moving faster than the water your indicator and flies are moving in. When this happens the fly line between you and the indicator moves faster than the indicator and creates a downstream belly in the line. The line tightens and starts to drag the flies and indicators down and across the current. The result is an un-natural drift. Mending the line is a way of removing the drag.

Mike took my rod and demonstrated how to mend the line. He lifted the rod to take out all the slack, then flipped the line upstream with a flick of the wrist. It was like a soft sideways roll cast. When he did this, the belly of the line lifted from the water and swung upstream without moving the strike indica-tor as it continued its drift downstream. The result was an up-stream loop in the line which slowly developed slack as the line moved faster than the indicator. There was no drag on the indicator or flies.

I tried, starting to get the hang of it in a few casts. In this swift current I had to make two or three upstream mends on each drift. I often had slack line but if I removed it, the flies would drag. The secret is to compromise. Make smaller more frequent mends to reduce the slack. After a day of mending I became reasonably competent…but several years later I still cannot mend with the smoothness and economy of motion Mike displayed that day.

Now that Mike had me mending, he explained that I needed to play out line at the lower part of the drift to cover more wa-ter per cast. He had me strip line off the reel and feed it through the rod onto the water in a small back and forth motion of the rod tip as the tip was pointing toward the drifting indicator. The line laid on the water in a snake-like pattern which slowly straightened as the downstream drift of the strike indicator took out line. The result was a much longer drag-free drift.

Mending and playing out line allowed me to cover far more water effectively. Using these techniques, it is possible to get a drag-free drift as long as the entire fly line. I find, however, that I do not like to use quite this long a drift. This is because having that long line out makes it difficult to set the hook prop-erly. On the end of a long drift I would miss strikes or loose fish shortly after a hookup. A shorter drift reduces those prob-lems.

Now I will place a 30– to 40–foot cast three-quartering up-stream and play out line until I have about twice as much line on the water at the downstream end of the drift. Then I take in half of the line and recast. This compromise allows proper line management and more success connecting with fish.

By the way, for some reason I get a large percentage of my strikes at the end of the drift. Deciding that I have allowed the flies to drift long enough, I begin to raise my rod to retrieve the extra line. I will find a fish on or I will feel a hit (often a miss) in that first instant of movement. Thinking it was the movement that did it, I have tried twitching the flies at other points on the drift with some success. I do not know what is happening to make the trout take the fly, but it seems to work. Later I learned this technique is called the Leisenring Lift.

## Nymphing Soft Waters

Nymphing is most successful in the large, swift currents of big western streams. Broad expanses of swift, fairly smooth water 2– to 4–feet deep are good candidates for use of the nymphing technique.

Like pocket water fishing, nymphing is most successful if you learn where the fish lie. Probably the most well known holding water for nymphing is where the current is diverted around some barrier. This barrier could be a rock, gravel bar, bend in the stream, a log, an old car, anything. The water speeds up as it goes around the barrier. The water directly below the barrier is slower. The result is a seam between the faster water and the slower water. This seam is where the food swept past the barrier starts to slow. Trout will station themselves in the slower water next to the seam and feed on what the current brings down to them.

This seam between fast and slow water is what I call soft water. Soft water can be found at the edges of runs, in the middle of riffles, on the edges of the stream, behind a sunken boulder or weed bed; anywhere the current speeds up by an obstruction, then spreads and slows.

### Riffles

Riffles are water areas with fast current running over rocks that cause the water to be choppy. They can be great places to nymph because if trout are in this fast water they are here to feed. However, they prefer to feed where they have some protection from the current. This protection is usually provided by submerged rocks on the bottom. The rock will break up the current and will also accelerate it as it passes over the rock. The result is an area of softer water on the bottom just behind the rock. Trout will hang in this softer water just below the fast current and wait for food to be swept by. They will rise into the fast current or move to the side into the current to feed, but will come back to the soft water to wait for the next morsel to present itself. This is the type of water I took the two 25–inchers from.

Perhaps a diagram will help to visualize what is happening here. In Figure 7–1 a rock is submerged in a riffle. The current sweeps over the top of it leaving a soft spot behind it. The trout rests in that spot just below the fast water. Submerged rock ledges, submerged logs, and weed beds cause this same break in the current.

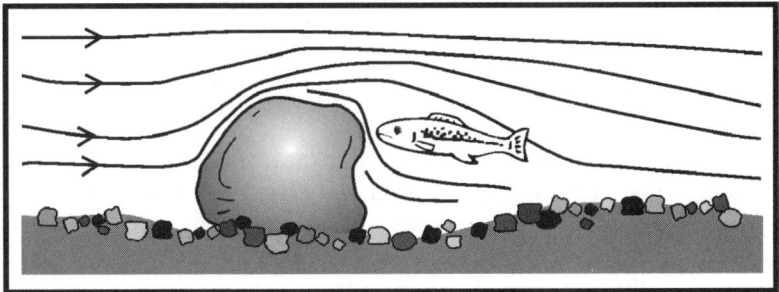

*Figure 7-1*
*Soft water behind a rock.*

Some of these soft water spots are visible as you fish. To fish them, cast your nymph rig above the object causing the break and allow it to drift over the break. The object is to get the flies to just miss hanging up on the top of the barrier. When the fly is at the right depth it will slow after it passes over the obstruction. That is usually the point where the take will occur. Trout seldom chase a fly downstream in this current because it costs so much energy to get back up to their holding spot.

To get the fly to just the right depth, adjust the weight and/ or the distance the fly lands above the obstruction. Start with less weight and a fairly close cast. If this doesn't work, cast more upstream to allow the flies more time to sink. If this still doesn't work, add weight.

Many of the fish-holding obstructions in riffles are not obvious from casting distance. However, there are areas in a riffle where the surface current is slower. Study the surface to find them. These slower areas suggest the presence of a barrier just upstream. Below the barrier is a bit deeper water. If there are no obvious areas of soft water, cover the riffle with general natural drifts. You may be rewarded.

Remember that riffles are usually shallow, sometimes only a few inches deep, yet they still hold good trout. Because of this shallow water, your strike indicator should be only 2– to 3–feet above the weight. Generally you will be using small weights so you will not need a large strike indicator. The smaller indicator is more sensitive to strikes and is less likely to spook a fish.

Also remember that trout in shallow water have a smaller field of vision because they are close to the surface. The flies need to be close to the fish for it to see them and react. In this shallow water you will need to make more casts to cover the water.

An alternative to the standard nymphing rig for shallow riffles is the dry fly and dropper rig. Use a buoyant dry and a dropper with a weighted body, a Beadhead Pheasant Tail for example. The dropper will be almost directly below the dry. In this way you can micro-manage the drift to prevent drag. A strike indicator that is 2–feet above a weight which is 1– to 3– feet above the flies can be in an entirely different current. The indicator could be drag free in fast water while it is dragging the flies through the soft water. Try the dry and dropper, especially in shallower riffles, and see if your success is not improved.

### Runs

Runs are slower, smoother, and usually deeper than riffles. In big western streams they can be more than 4–feet deep, long, and quite fast. Trout must have a reason to hold in a run. Again the reason is a break in the current which provides a holding area near a good food source. Look for seams where a faster

***Good nymphing run. Pay particular attention to the seam
between the two water flows.***

current meets a slower one. Also look for bubbles. They indicate a current that is often rich in food. A seam of soft water
with bubbles is an ideal place to drift your nymphs.

Trout are usually feeding near the bottom in runs. Pay particular attention to getting the flies down. In clear western
streams, a run that looks 2–feet deep may actually be 6–feet
deep or more. If the weight is not occasionally bumping the
bottom...once every two or three casts...it is not deep enough.
Add weight and/or lengthen the distance between the indicator and the weight. Also, when I use heavy weight I like to
lengthen the tippet below the weight. This allows the flies to
move more naturally in the small current changes without being tugged by the weight.

## Pools

Pools are the type of water that many fly fishers head to first
when nymphing. They can be productive if fished correctly. A
pool consists of a head where a swift current empties into it, a
deep slow body, and a tail with increasing current that rises
from the bottom as the pool becomes shallow. Fish will be concentrated in a few areas.

At the head of a pool is a classic seam of soft water, usually at the edges on both sides. As the current breaks over whatever barrier causes the pool, the current slows and spreads. The seam at the edges just below the barrier will hold trout. Often the pool will have a back eddy. Fish the seam as it slows into the deep water of the pool. Fish will suspend a foot or so below the surface in this slower current. Try the dry and dropper for these suspended fish *and* the nymph rig for the fish that are feeding either downstream and/or at deeper levels. In this area fish are not always on the bottom.

The body of a pool is deep and slow. Fish are sometimes there. If they are, they are likely not to be feeding. I do not spend time on an unobstructed pool body with an even bottom. However, if there is something to cause trout to be attracted, it is a different story. Large rocks, even though they do not provide current breaks, attract fish. A tree overhanging the pool provides shade and potential terrestrial food and can be a great place for brown trout, even in the bright midday sun.

Undercut banks act like overhangs. They provide a shaded hiding place for fish to spring from. Nymph as close to the bank as possible with a fairly long leader. If conditions are right, the current may take the flies under the bank. Prepare for a strike as this is a favorite hiding place, especially for bigger trout.

The tail-out of a pool is where the water shallows and speeds up on its way to the next riffle or run. Fish will often hold here and feed on the bugs brought up by the up-swelling current. Sometimes they will be in such shallow water that their backs are out of water. This is a particularly favorite spot for brook trout.

Tail-out trout are more spooky than most and will bolt for the deeper body of the pool if frightened. Sometimes all that is needed to cause this reaction is a false cast or even the thought of one. Still these are actively feeding fish which should not be ignored.

I much prefer upstream approaches in almost all fly fishing situations. But in this case a downstream presentation can be the only way to not spook the fish. Use a small strike indicator, a fairly long length between the indicator and the weight (6–

feet or so), a light weight, and a long tippet. Also, expect to miss a lot of takes. Just remember, one fish on the line is probably better than you would have done if you had approached from downstream.

## Flies

The typical nymph is the larval or immature worm-like stage of a mayfly, caddis fly, or midge. Size and color varies with the bugs that are active at the time. Ask at the local fly shop and/or look under stream bottom rocks to get ideas. It is rare that you will need anything beyond the Pheasant Tail, Prince, and Western Midge Emerger I have outlined in Chapter 5.

Without local knowledge, I start on free-stone streams with a No. 16 Beadhead Prince and a No. 20 Flash Pheasant Tail behind it. They seem to imitate the size and color of the naturals in most western streams.

On tailwaters my starting rig is a No. 20 Flash Pheasant Tail and a No. 24 gray Western Midge Emerger.

During spawning seasons in spring and fall I will use an egg pattern for the top fly. When the blue wing olives (BWO) are in season—winter to early spring and again in late fall—I will use the green and gray BWO colors in a No. 18 emerger.

## The Wet Fly Swing

Sometimes incredibly effective, the wet fly swing is an old technique that has gone out of fashion but still works. I learned this technique from guide Jim Suttleworth (888–487–4500) on the Yakima River in Washington. Jim explained that it works great for fish that are feeding on emergers. It works particularly well on trout that are feeding in riffles and runs where there is no obvious hatch.

The rig is simple...two nymphs or wet flies tied to the line as in the nymph rig. No weight or indicator is used. A 5X tippet is usually the lightest you can get away with as the trout hit the fly hard on a tight line. Often a 4X is better.

The flies to use are dependant on the bug activity, but some general flies work most of the time. A simple wet fly can be made by lightly dubbing the shank of a hook with Antron in one of the common emerger colors. Also try red or orange. Then add a sparse collar of soft hackle, hence the fly is called a Soft Hackle. It can be tied with or without a beadhead. Alternatively an un-weighted No. 16 Prince Nymph works well as the top fly. The bottom fly can be a smaller Flash Pheasant Tail, a No. 20 Western Midge Emerger, or a La Fontaine Deep Sparkle Pupa. Experiment. I have found that most nymphs work; some better than others.

To fish the wet fly swing, position yourself on the shore side and upstream of the area to be fished. Cast somewhat down-stream and across. The cast should be positioned so that there is little or no slack as the flies start their swing. Usually a cast three-quarters downstream does the trick. Without any slack, the flies will stay near the surface which is just where you want them.

As the line floats downstream, hold onto the line so that none slips from your hand. This will cause the flies to swing across the water in an arch. Point your rod tip toward the flies and follow it downstream. Continue to follow the swing until the flies are directly downstream. Let them swing in the current

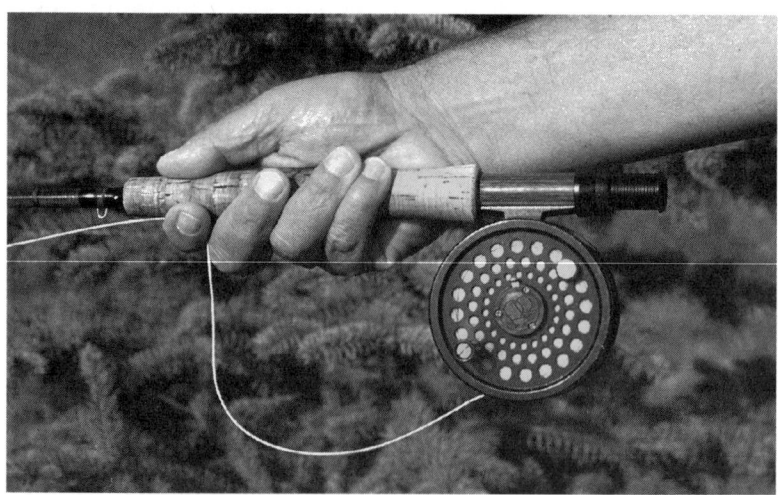

*Slack needed so fish will not break off when they hit a*
*wet fly swing.*

for a few seconds. Finally strip in about half your line in short jerks. Then recast the full length of line.

Select a line length that gets to the water you wish to cover but not so long that it takes a lot of casting to get it out. Shorter is better. This technique works best for me if my line is short enough that I can lift it from the water, swing my position at the backcast and lay the line upstream at the correct angle in one solid motion without any false casts. In this way I can cover the water effectively and quickly without a lot of extra work.

Trout hit the fly on the swing or as it straightens below you. Be prepared, hits are often violent. To succeed in hooking more fish, you must build a little slack into your line to absorb the impact. Do this by allowing a small loop of fly line to extend from the reel to your index finger on the handle of the rod. (See Photo.) Place the line between your index finger and the cork handle. Put just enough pressure on the line to prevent slipping; no more. Do not touch the line with your non-casting hand. Set the drag on your reel only tight enough to prevent an overrun or backlash, but no more. In other words, use almost no drag.

When the trout hits, it will hook itself or it will miss. If it is hooked, it will pull the loop of line through your index finger. Do not lift the rod. Instead, catch the line with your non-casting hand and stop further line from going out. This will set the hook. Be ready to quickly release the line if it is a big fish. Otherwise it may break the tippet because there is no longer any shock absorbing play in the line or the rod. Once the fish is hooked and on the reel, raise the rod tip and play it as you would any other.

Expect to miss a few fish. Hits from small fish can be numerous and you will miss most of them. The bigger fish, however, are less likely to miss. You will learn not to clamp down on the line too much once you have broken off a few good ones!

This is a searching technique. Often you cannot see the fish working in a riffle. To cover the water completely, start at the upstream shoreline edge of the riffle. If the water bends, fish the inside edge where there is slower water. Select a casting distance that is comfortable to handle. Cast into the fast current and let the swing take the flies to the slower inside current. Make a couple of casts and swings. Then move downstream two steps. Make two more casts and move another two steps downstream. Do not move too far. The idea is to cover all the water. A trout may not see a fly that is more than two feet in front of it in the shallow water you are most likely to be fishing with this technique.

One of the beauties of the wet fly swing is that it requires very little active attention. Cast. Hold the rod in your casting hand and follow the swing. After a while it will become automatic. This gives you time to notice the wildflowers in bloom halfway up the slope across the river. It is a very pleasant, as well as effective, way to fish the riffles and runs of large rivers, but it works well on smaller streams too. I find myself working up a stream using a dry and dropper or standard nymph rig. Then if I have not had great success, I will re-fish the same water back downstream with the wet fly swing. It is amazing how many fish I will pick up on the return downstream.

Well, there you have the basics of nymphing on western streams. It can be great fun and often far more productive than fishing with dry flies. True, the rig is a little more cumbersome than a dry, but nymphing is fishing to trout the way they feed 80 percent of the time. Once you are practiced at it, the added fish will more than compensate for the inconvenience of the rig.

# Chapter 8

# *Stripping Streamers*

The streamer landed right next to a big boulder on shore. I pointed my fly rod at it and started stripping in line rapidly. Suddenly the water exploded. I jumped in surprise and forgot to set the hook. The fish was on the fly for a couple of seconds thrashing and churning the water...then it was gone.

I have fly fished for northern pike (see Chapter 14) and this was just the kind of savage take they are known for. But it wasn't a pike. Doing its best imitation of this legend predator was a big trout.

Roger Rehurek, guide and an owner of Cottonwood Camp on the Big Horn River in Montana (406–666–2391), had promised me a day of exceptional fun and big fish. I took his offer like a yearling rainbow full of enthusiasm and covered with parr marks. He didn't even need to set the hook. It was truly an exceptional experience.

Trout are known primarily as bug eaters. However, as they get bigger their tastes turn to bigger bites. Minnows, leaches, crawfish, etc. become a more important item in their diet. Streamers imitate minnows. Woolly Buggers imitate leaches, minnows, or nothing at all. Streamers, especially Woolly Buggers, are an important part of your fly arsenal.

## *Equipment*

Streamers are usually fairly big flies. Size 10 long shank hooks are small for streamers. Size 2– to 6– are common. These large flies require a heavy rod to move them through the air. I use my 7–weight but the 5–weight will work; it is just a little cumbersome.

Trout hit streamers hard most of the time. Fine leaders will break on the take or as the hook is set. I never use less than 3X tippet. More frequently I will use 0X and even 20 pound mono. In streamer stripping the trout are not usually leader shy. Tapered leaders are not needed because the weight of the fly will extend the leader but you do need a stiff leader to turn the fly over. Try

30 pound Maxima with a 20 pound Stren tippet or cut back a tapered 7½ foot 0X and add tippet of 20 pound Stren if a heavy tippet is needed. If you are fishing lighter leader material like 2X, cut back the tapered leader some and add 2 feet of 2X. This will give you a very effective leader. Leader length is dependent on the water fished. It could be as short as 6 feet or up to 12 feet, 6 feet of tapered leader and 2 feet of 2X tipper is my standard starting rig.

Often streamers are weighted to get them down into deeper waters. Some fly fishers will add weight above the fly. Others will use sinking tip lines or sinking tips added to floating lines to help get the streamer down to the fish. I hate sinking tips and will use them only under duress. When I do, I use the add-on sinking tips available by Orvis or Cortland. This eliminates the need for changing lines. Just add the sinking tip loop-to-loop to the end of the floating fly line and you are ready to go. The add-on tips come in different lengths and sink rates so they are actually more flexible than sinking lines.

## *Techniques*

### *Swing and Strip*

The classic streamer drift starts with a three-quarters upstream cast. Allow the fly to sink as it drifts downstream taking up some of the slack line as it does. When it is downstream from you, take in the remaining slack. As the line tightens the fly will start to lift from the bottom and swing across the stream. Strip in small amounts of line as it swings. This will impart a natural swimming motion to the fly. Keep the rod tip down and pointed toward the fly.

The fly will probably swing all the way downstream below you as you retrieve it. As it straightens, be prepared, the end of the swing often generates a strike. Baring this, continue stripping the line until the fly is less than two rod lengths below you. Strikes can come at any time as trout will follow the streamer. A smashing strike close up can get your heart pumping.

Vary the retrieve. Long strips, short strips, pauses, slow and steady, or dead-drift swings. They are all effective at times. Any retrieve that makes the trout believe in the fly is good.

Cover the water with several casts at different distances from shore in a fan shape. When the water has been covered, move downstream a few feet and cover the new water. I usually start with casts close to me, then work out into the main current and beyond it toward the other bank. Pay particular attention to any seams, bubble lines, or stream obstructions as these may hold fish.

## Strip Set

Setting the hook on a streamer strike takes practice. The tendency is to raise the rod as you would any other take. This doesn't work. The fish is on for a few seconds, then gone.

To set the hook successfully on streamer strikes use the strip set. To accomplish the strip set keep your rod tip down near the water and pointed at the fly. When the trout wacks the fly, tighten the line with a quick strip of line and hold the line tight. At this point whatever you do, *do not lift your rod tip*. The trout will be thrashing at the end of your line. Keep the tip of the rod pointed at the fish and the line tight. There is no slack in your line and no bend to your rod at this point which is why those heavy tippets are needed to prevent breaking off. Once the trout starts to swim, give or take line as needed and slowly raise the rod.

The reason the strip set is necessary makes sense once you think about it. A big trout has just engulfed the fly. The streamer is now deep in its mouth, locked behind clenched jaws. The first tension you feel is the line against the jaws. No pressure is put on the fly. Without a hard set, the trout struggles for a while then opens its mouth and spits out the fly. The strip set pulls the leader through the trout's mouth and forces the hook into its jaw. Fish on!

Roger taught me the strip set. Before we started that first drift down the Big Horn he explained it. He then said that most fly fishers miss the first five to ten fish before they learn not to raise the rod tip on the strike. I was about average. The point gets driven home when the eighth 16– to 18–inch trout escapes because of an improper set!

## The Two-Fly Rig

I was on the Colorado River one day fishing one of the long runs that section of the river is famous for but without success. I had nymphed it with everything I could think of. I could not believe that there were no fish, so I kept trying. Finally in desperation I thought a Woolly Bugger might work. I put on a black one but was too lazy to remove the strike indicator. Fast strips, slow strips, nothing worked until I tried a dead-drift. I got a bump just at the end of the drift as the Woolly Bugger started to lift and swing. A few casts later I got another bump…no fish, but an improvement.

Then I thought, suppose the Woolly Bugger is acting like an attractor fly. I tied on a dropper Beadhead Prince. The next cast yielded a nice 14–inch brown on the Prince on the dead-drift. Several casts later another brown hit the Woolly Bugger just as it started to swing.

Since that day I have used this combination on several occasions. The best water for it appears to be long, fairly deep runs. The dead-drift will generally produce on the Prince while the swing and strip upstream brings the Woolly Bugger more into play. By the way, use a fairly heavy tippet for the dropper; 4X or even 3X. This is because of an unusual problem. It is not easy to tell if the fish is taking the Woolly Bugger or the Prince, so I strip set all takes. Light tippet produces lots of broken off Prince nymphs.

## Streamer Water

### Runs

The water I find most conducive to successful streamer stripping are the long, deep, fairly fast runs that are found in classic large western rivers. These waters are 2– to 6–feet deep. The current is fairly fast and steady. Seams and structure breaks, usually boulders, add character to the flow and holding places for the trout.

I start at the top of such runs and work my way downstream. If you can, wade out far enough that the end of the downstream swing and upstream retrieve are in about 2 feet or more of water. To get a better drift, try going out further into the current after you have covered the closer water. Once the farther water has been covered, move back toward shore before moving downstream and repeating the process to cover new water.

### Pools

The slow, deep water of a pool can hide some big fish. I am not always successful at dredging one up out of a pool, but it works often enough to make the effort worthwhile. Streams known to hold large trout (above 14–inches) are your best bet. Early and late in the day will find the fish more in a feeding mood.

### Undercut Banks

This is a great way to get some big fish. Try to get the streamer to drift under the bank. Use slight strips so that the fly has movement but is not pulled out from the bank.

## Floating the Banks

Drifting down a river and stripping streamers off the bank, as I did on the Big Horn, can be spectacular. Cast to likely-looking structure with a weighted streamer. Look for boulders, logs, overhanging trees and current seams. Immediately start stripping the fly and hang on. Strikes will come in the first one to four strips. Keep your retrieve short because fish seldom go far from their holding areas to chase these fast moving streamers. Several short retrieves will be more productive than one long one.

*Guide Roger Rehurek and Harley with Big Horn*
*rainbow taken on a streamer.*

## Flies

Streamers are usually designed to imitate minnows or small trout. The muddler minnow is the most commonly found minnow in western streams.

The most well-known muddler imitation is called the Muddler Minnow Pattern. It is made from deer hair with a fat head. I have had limited success with it. It does not sink well unless heavily weighted and has very little movement.

There are several alternative patterns made with marabou and other softer materials that have far more life-like action. Most are weighted with dumbbell eyes. Choose one that appeals to you. They are all about equally successful.

To imitate a trout fry, use a lighter colored streamer. Again there are numerous alternatives that are equally effective. Chose one you like and have confidence in. If you believe in it, you will fish it with confidence and be successful with it.

Woolly Buggers should be the mainstay of any fly fisher's streamer box. If you have only one streamer in your box, this should be it. The black with peacock cactus chenille I discussed in Chapter 5 is my mainstay. I also use olive, brown, purple, fuchsia, and white; either weighted with a bead or conehead or un-weighted. A selection of colors in a small (No. 8 to No. 10) and a large size (No. 2 to No. 6) will be all you need in most western waters. Select the color and size which best matches the forage fish in the water and you are in business. When in doubt, use black.

Streamer stripping is not always productive, but when you are on a stream with a lot of big fish (over 14–inches), this technique can produce a truly memorable day. One of the best times to use it is in early fall when the browns are in pre-spawn and are aggressive. It is a big fish technique so don't expect any small trout. However, I have caught trout as small as 6–inches on streamers. They were given a heroism award and released gently in hopes of finding them and their feistiness again in a few years. The smashing strike of a big fish with attitude makes this a technique I come back to again and again.

*Keith Keenan with a fish he hooked just off the bank.*

# Chapter 9

## Fishing On The Edge

My Parachute Adams settled just inches from shore. As it bounced lightly on the current, a giant nose slowly broke the surface, a mouth opened and my fly disappeared. I set the hook and a torpedo decided that the shallow water was not the place to be. She slugged it out deep under the boat. Finally a beautiful 21–inch brown came to net, the best of many that day. I was fishing the Green River at Flaming Gorge, Utah with my guide Pat Nichols (801–971–4180). Never once that day did we fish the deep water runs where most of the fly fishers and guides were nymphing. We were fishing on the edge.

The concept of fishing on the edge was crystallized in my mind by a simple comment. I was in Salida, Colorado to fish the Arkansas River and, never having fished the area before, stopped at Arkansas River Fly Shop (719–539–3474) for advice. In discussing where and how to fish, Rod Patch, the owner, made a casual observation which really struck home. "You know," he said, "most fly fishers stand where they should be fishing." He then explained that most fly fishers charge into the water to nymph the middle of the runs. Instead, he suggested, they should fish the little pockets on the edge of the stream where the current is broken by rocks and boulders.

Armed with the thought of fishing on the edge, I began to explore. On the edge of the big, fast runs typical of the Arkansas were numerous pockets of relatively calm water. A careful approach along the rocks and a short cast to avoid drag presented the fly to the fish in those pockets. During the blue-wing olive hatch they came up to a dry. When there was no hatch, they took an emerger. I observed that others were, indeed, standing in the type of water where I was catching fish. To make matters worse, they were nymphing the runs with little success. Thanks to Rod's suggestion, my altered approach turned a potential disaster into three days of great fun.

A bit of thought reveals why this strategy is effective. Trout do not like to waste energy fighting fast water. They prefer slower—but not dead slow—water if it supplies them with protection and food.

## Fish Holding Areas

There are several types of shoreline structure which hold fish. These include shoreline breaks, overhangs, weeds and undercut banks, whirlpools and pool shoulders. Each has its unique opportunities to catch trout. Almost none are deep. It is amazing how many good fish can be found in a foot or so of water. These shallow water trout are usually feeding actively.

*This bush forms a small pocket fish love.*

### Shoreline Breaks

Boulders, fallen logs, sweepers, rock ledges and bridge abutments that project into faster currents are prime fish holding areas. (See Figures 9–1, 9–2, 9–3.) They cause a break in the flow where fish find protection from the current and easy meals. Look for seams on the edge of the break nearest the main current. The water on the shoreline side of the seam should be fairly smooth, not boiling, as this rough water wastes a trout's energy. Fish are found in the seam between the fast and slow water just below the break.

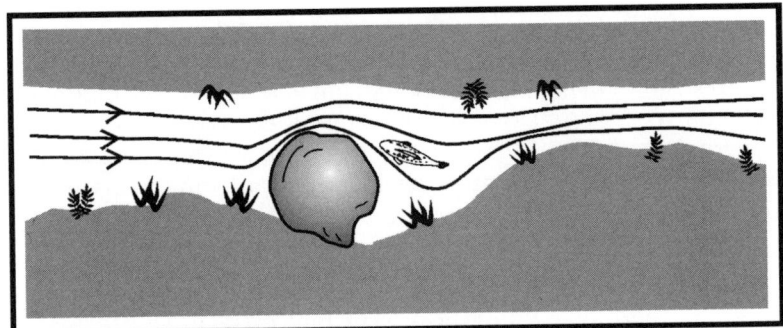

*Figure 9–1   Shoreline rock structure.*

*Figure 9-2   Fish locations at shoreline log.*

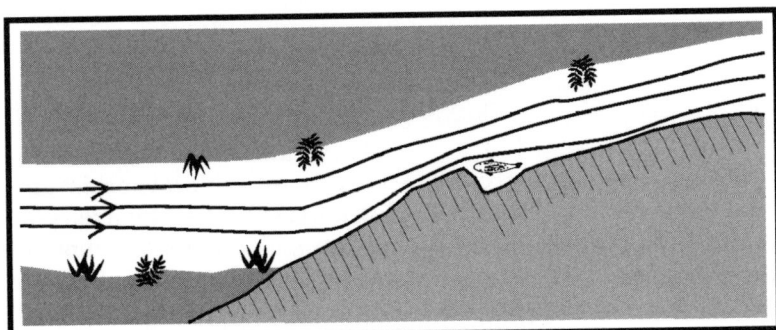

*Figure 9–3   Pocket on rock wall.*

## Overhangs, Undercut Banks and Weeds

Trout prefer the shade and overhead protection of overhanging trees and bushes. They also like the insects which congregate in them. When the current is not too fast or too slow, and the overhang not too far above the water, these areas can produce great action. Protective overhangs can be fairly far from the main current or deeper water but are better fish holders if some deep water is near for the fish to hide in if threatened.

Undercut banks provide similar overhead protection and access to food. (See Figure 9–4.) The best areas are at the lower end of a bend where the water shallows and slows. Undercuts

*Figure 9-4   Fish holding under bank.*

in the middle of the bend where there is fast, boiling water are usually not productive.

Shoreline weeds can create an overhang similar to an undercut bank. I recall one trout who lived in such a habitat. He came out just far enough to sip spinners an inch outside the edge of the weed. Two inches was too far. After several casts I finally got it just right and was rewarded with a nice 18–inch brown.

## Whirlpools and Pool Shoulders

When the main current enters a pool, the water slows. Sometimes it produces a whirlpool or backwater where the water circles toward shore and back upstream. My 21–inch brown was in just such a whirlpool facing downstream in the reversed current right next to shore. Getting a good drift can be tricky. I find it best to fish toward shore in these circumstances. Fish the normal downstream current seam first, then fish across it to the upward flowing backwater. Use a short cast and keep your line off the water to prevent drag from the downstream current.

Even when the water does not produce a whirlpool, there will be a slow water pocket at the edge of the fast water just as it enters the pool This shoulder area is produced on one or both sides of the pool. It almost always contains a trout or two. (See Figure 9–5.)

Sometimes trout are near shore in open shallow water without any apparent structure to attract them. If you see one and its dorsal fin is up, it is feeding, probably on small nymphs. A careful cast, angled so you don't line it, will get results. (See Chapter 10.)

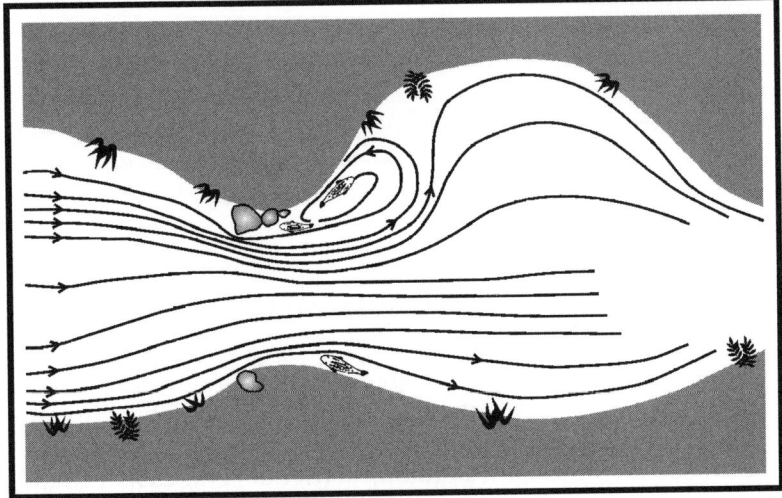

***Figure 9–5   Fish feeding in whirlpool (top) and
shoulder of pool.***

## *Technique*

The technique for fishing on the edge is derived from pocket water fishing. Use a floating line and a short leader of 6– to 8–feet. Fish with two flies. When there is no hatch use an attractor dry. My favorite is a No. 12 Coachman Trude. For the dropper use a general nymph, either a Beadhead Brassie or a Beadhead Prince. Of course, if there is a hatch on or if there is the promise of one, use a dry and an emerger that matches it at least generally in size, shape and color. During terrestrial (summer into fall) season use a grasshopper or ant as the dry if the Coachman Trude does not work.

In most instances you will want to keep the length of your dropper tippet fairly short. Start with about two feet. If you are not getting down near the bottom add some length. If you are catching the bottom frequently, shorten your dropper. Experiment to find a length that works.

Keep in mind that a perfectly placed dry fly will have a dropper fly landing somewhere else. If the ideal areas are small, a long dropper will miss them. On the other hand, a beadhead lands with a plop. If this plop is close to your dry, it could scare away your fish. Practice will teach you the best compromise for each situation.

Once you have picked your spot, approach from downstream and fish upstream. In shoreline break situations and in whirlpools and pool shoulders, employ a short cast, seldom more than 20 feet. The primary purpose of the short cast is to prevent line drag. Hold your rod high to keep as much of the line off the water as possible. It is not uncommon for only my leader to be on the water.

Cast to the seam where the water slowed by the shoreline obstruction joins the faster water. Precision casting is often necessary. Six inches to one side and you are in the fast water. The fly is out of the fish's field of vision before it can react. Six inches to the other side and the flies just sit there, unnaturally still or stuck on the shore. As the flies drift down with the current, lift your rod to avoid drag. You will get only a few seconds of drag-free drift but that is all you will need. Watching your fly's movement and noting where you catch fish will teach you where to present your fly. Two or three properly placed casts will tell whether a fish is at home and hungry. If not, move up to the next break in the current. Frequent short drifts are the most effective way to cover this type of water.

In overhang and undercut bank situations a longer cast may be needed. With a slow, quiet approach you will not spook the fish. The current muffles sound. The upstream approach means you are in the fish's blind spot. It is usually not necessary, however, to crawl or crouch to keep the fish from seeing you. Do avoid splashing or making waves as this surely will spook your quarry. Also, wear neutral colors that blend in with your background, making yourself less obvious to the trout.

## *Big Water and Small*

Fishing on the edge is effective in big, fast streams and in small, relatively slow ones.

The Roaring Fork in Colorado is aptly named. From the time the Frying Pan River adds its flow, the Fork picks up speed and volume through the valley until it joins the Colorado River at Glenwood Springs. This river is traditionally fished by floating. The rower is always busy keeping the boat in position and off the rocks as the boat roars down the river with the current. When fishing this river I use guide Craig Davis of the Frying Pan Anglers (970–927–3441). He keeps the boat in position as well as anyone I have experienced.

The fly fisher is kept busy too. This is the fastest fishing on the edge you are likely to experience. Cast. Drift for a few seconds, then your fly is dragging. Recast ten or more feet down river to the next shoreline pocket that will allow you a few seconds of natural drift. It is frustrating because you cannot cover more than a few of the likely looking pockets. If you hook a branch just break the fly off. There is no going back in this current. If you hook a fish, don't expect much help from the rower, he or she is too busy.

It is a lot of work, but the effort is repaid when a chunky brown or rainbow splats your dry or chases your nymph. I am amazed when I get a chance to think about it—which is usually two or three days later once my mind and heart have slowed—how many really nice size fish live in those shoreline pockets just beside that roaring current. In this water you need a large fly to convince the fish that chasing it will be worthwhile. The most common combination is a No. 10 Parachute Grasshopper (in the hopper season) or a large Stimulator and a No. 12 Beadhead Pheasant Tail. The sight of a broad-backed trout coming almost out of the water to get your fly before it gets away downstream is truly exciting. Here fishing on the edge is the only place you can fish successfully.

Casting a big streamer toward  the shore as I did on the Big Horn (see Chapter 8) can also be effective on these big fast waters.

The effectiveness of fishing on the edge is not restricted to large rivers with swift currents. The technique is just as effective in smaller streams. Imagine a long run in a small stream. The water moves nicely between two lines of willows then bends against a rocky shore. The run is only two feet deep and not too swift to fish. Most fly fishers will nymph a run like this and ignore the shoreline structure on its edge. But that is not the best way to fish it. Just like in larger streams, the fish wish to avoid the extra work of living in the faster water. Look for the sometimes subtle current breaks and overhangs where the fast water of the run meets the shoreline. While fish may be in the middle of the run if they are attracted by an abundant food source such as hatching flies, when an easy meal is not present they will live in the relative calm of those shoreline current breaks. The fish will be actively feeding in the run for only brief periods each day. The rest of the time they will feed opportunistically from their holds on the edge.

As an experiment I fished one such run by both nymphing the run and fishing the edge with a dry and dropper. I caught 14 rainbows on the edge and one in the run. Most of the time the odds are better on the edge.

NOTE:  A version of this chapter appeared in *American Angler* (November/December, 1999) p.27.

# Chapter 10

## Sight Fishing

Perhaps some ancient hunting instinct is still left in me. I love the challenge of spotting a trout and having it take my fly. This is called *sight fishing* and it is one of the most rewarding techniques I know of in fly fishing.

*Brown visibly feeding on nymphs*

All of us have done some sight fishing. Rising trout tell you where they are by their rise. You have sighted them even if you cannot see them in the water. A good presentation of a reasonable imitation should produce a fish.

The sight fishing I am talking about is a little different. The fish are feeding subsurface so there is no hint on the surface. Finding them can sometimes prove quite a challenge. Catching them can be another considerable task. The feeling one experiences when your efforts result in a fish is a large part of what fly fishing is all about.

Sight fishing consists of three separate skills: sighting a fish, determining what it is feeding on, and presenting the proper fly correctly to get a take without spooking the fish. Each is a special skill that takes practice to master.

## Sight Fishing Waters

Sight fishing works best in shallow water or in a few rare cases where trout are suspended in the upper part of deeper water. Shallow riffles are ideal locations. The fish will hold behind slight current breaks. It requires a fair amount of energy for the trout to keep in position so a fish is not likely to be in this fast water unless it is actively feeding.

Slower, deeper runs can hold visible fish. Look for them at the shallow edges. They could also be suspended anywhere in the run that brings them lots of food, so look for them in seams where you might fish a nymph.

I have often seen pods of trout suspended in the deep water of a pool, especially a backwater or whirlpool. They are easy to spot. That is the good news. It is difficult to correctly judge the depth they are holding in. That's the bad news. In clear western stream these suspended fish are likely to be deeper than they appear to be, so adjust accordingly.

Sight fishing in lakes and ponds can be very effective. However, the rules are somewhat different. Stillwater sight fishing to shoreline cruisers will be covered in Chapter 13, Lakes and Ponds,

## Sighting Fish

Sighting trout in a stream or lake can be extraordinarily difficult. When you are out with a guide or other practiced fish spotter it can be truly frustrating. This has happened to me on numerous occasions. My companion will spot a fish and tell me it is at a specific location. I will stare, squint, search and shrug. I can't see a thing! However, after some practice—and usually after spooking several fish—I start seeing them.

I do not know any great secret that makes spotting trout suspended in a stream easy, but there are a few things which can make it easier.

First, get yourself the best pair of polarized sunglasses you can. I have used expensive clip-ons with success. However, just recently I purchased a pair of prescription polarized sunglasses and the difference is amazing. Some people swear by the brown color...others the green...others the gray. Experiment to find out which works best for you. A pair of sunglasses which allow you to focus precisely and penetrate the glare of the light on the water surface are essential to success. Even if you don't need visual correction, do not skimp on Polaroids. The good ones have carefully contoured hard lenses that eliminate distortion and make spotting fish easier.

Second, do not focus on the surface or the bottom. Try to focus on the water column in between. This is a trick which takes some practice. If you focus on the bottom or the surface, your vision will not be as sharp in the middle of the water column where the fish are, making them harder to spot.

Third, look for out-of-place shapes, movements or shadows. Often my first clue is a shadow on the bottom. Sometimes I will see movement, a flash of light on the fish's side, a speck of white as the trout's mouth opens to take a bug.

Sighting a fish is often an amazing experience. I will be looking at a run seeing nothing. Then, all of a sudden, a fish will appear out of nowhere. It was there all the time, of course, but by looking at the water just right the non-fish items will fade into the background like a Bev Doolittle painting. To see the hidden image you must not focus on the detail. Like anything else, the more you do it, the easier it becomes.

## Reading the Fish

Once a fish has been spotted, it is necessary to determine if it is feeding and how it is feeding. A lot can be learned from watching a fish for a few minutes. Don't cast to a fish the instant you spot it. A little study can add significantly to your success.

Chuck Rizuto, owner of Rizuto's Lodge and Fly Shop at Navaho Dam (505–632–1411) on the San Juan in New Mexico, taught me how to read a trout's feeding behavior. One four-hour session was like a Ph.D. in fish behavior. I recommend it if you have the chance.

He taught me to observe how the fish is behaving. Is it sitting in one location without any motion? Is it's dorsal fin down? Is its body even with the water, head neither up or down? If so, it is probably not feeding. No amount of casting is likely to get such a fish to take your offering.

An actively feeding fish will move. Sometimes the movement is only slight. It will move purposefully to the right or left. Its mouth will open with a wink of white and it will re-station itself in the original or some other resting area. After a few minutes observation, the fish's feeding range will become apparent.

Now observe how its head is held. If the head is down, the trout is feeding on nymphs near the bottom. If the head is up, it is feeding on emergers rising toward the surface.

Reading a fish teaches us a lot about how to catch it. We know where in the water column to present the fly. We know what general type of fly the trout is feeding on. Even without knowledge of currently active bugs, we can make an educated guess as to what the fish is keying into. We are now ready to rig up and present a fly to the fish.

## *Presentation*

The object of the presentation is to make your fly look as much like the real thing as possible. This means that the fly should drift to the trout with the same speed as the current. It should be at the level the trout is feeding in when it reaches the visual range of the fish. Also, it should be close enough to the fish so it will be spotted. Remember that a trout's visual cone depends upon how deep the water is. Shallow water reduces its visual cone, necessitating a more accurate cast. And, of course, the fly should be presented so that the line does not spook the fish.

Getting the fly to the right depth requires a combination of proper weight and the proper cast. The fly will sink slowly as it drifts with the current. It will sink faster with more weight. The fly will have sunk deeper if it has drifted a further distance. Flies act more natural if they have less weight in front of them. It would seem the solution to getting them to deep holding fish would be simple, just cast further upstream. But there is a potential problem—isn't there always? The longer the drift, the more likely it is that conflicting currents will take the fly away from its intended target or cause unnatural drag.

The solution is a compromise between a longer cast and more weight...thus a shorter cast. In the fairly regular currents of deeper runs and pools, the longer cast is the better solution. In fast riffles more weight and shorter casts will work best.

## The Rig

In most cases visible fish will be feeding on nymphs or emergers in shallow water. Chuck showed me the rig he uses. It is quite standard ...two small emergers and a small weight. The first fly is about 18 inches below the weight and the second is about a foot behind the first. This makes a compact unit.

Chuck does not use a strike indicator. He feels that the fish see it coming before they see the flies and are wary of the flies. In shallow, clear water where it is easy to see the fish, I agree. But in deeper water or in light conditions where it is not as easy to see the fish, a *very* small strike indicator has proven helpful. I will use a short, single strand of yarn. Not enough to hold the flies up, just enough that you can see any unnatural movement in the line. I position it about two feet above the weight if fishing in shallow water; further up if the fish are in deeper water.

## The Cast

To keep current and drag problems at a minimum, try to keep your casts as short as possible. Approach the trout from behind and slightly to one side to take advantage of their blind spot. It is amazing to me how close one can get to an actively feeding fish with a slow approach. Try to use streamside brush and trees to disguise your outline. Wear medium hue, dull clothes and hat. I even avoid chromed equipment like forceps and nippers. Some fly fishers crouch or even crawl. I have found this very rarely necessary, only when there is no vegetation on the bank. Approach in a series of stop and goes. Stop and observe, then approach some more until you are close enough to make a controlled short cast. Once you are in position, don't cast immediately. Instead observe the fish for a few minutes. This will tell you about its feeding pattern and depth. It will also allow the fish to settle down if it has been alerted by your approach.

False cast as little as possible and definitely *not* over the trout. If the fish becomes agitated because of your cast, just stand there without motion. Wait until the fish resumes feeding; a minute, five minutes. It is amazing how long five minutes can seem. Just remember that it will take far more time to find and approach another fish! Don't fidget and wave your rod around. Don't talk loudly. Do observe. I often find a second or even a third fish in the area I did not see initially.

Don't cast to the trout while it is still agitated. It will not feed anyway and it will probably get even more scared, eliminating any chance you had to get it. Wait until the trout has resumed feeding.

Once the fish has settled down and is actively feeding, make your cast. The cast should be upstream and somewhat to the right or left, depending on your position relative to the fish. This angle will help keep the fly line from passing within the trout's cone of vision before the flies reach it.

## The Set

Chuck and I were fishing a shallow riffle where trout were feeding in less than two feet of water. We could see them fairly easily. Chuck positioned me about 20 feet below and 10 feet to the right of an actively feeding rainbow. He told me to set the hook with a gentle rod lift any time I saw the fish move or open its mouth.

I cast a few feet upstream from the fish and lifted my rod as the line and fly drifted down toward her to prevent slack and drag. I could not see the flies but I could estimate their progress and I could see the fish. The rainbow made a very slight move to the right. I watched, waiting for a take. Chuck asked me if I saw the movement. I said yes. Then he asked why I didn't set the hook. I said I didn't think the fish took the fly. Chuck then patiently explained the technique again.

The takes on these small flies are often quite subtle. By the time the fly fisher would feel the take, the fish would have taken and spit out the fly. In fact, most times the fly fisher never feels the take. A strike indicator, even if it did not scare the fish, would also be too slow to indicate most takes. To succeed in hooking trout that are actively nymphing in shallow riffles, set the hook at the slightest *hint* of a take. A *hint* includes slight movements and the wink of an opening mouth.

Armed with renewed resolve, I cast again to the rainbow. Several casts later the fish again moved slightly. I set the hook. No fish. Chuck said the rainbow took a natural but that I had the right idea. Two casts later the same subtle movement produced a solid hookup and a beautiful 16–inch rainbow with vibrant red sides.

## Patience and Innovation

Patience and sometimes innovation are required in sight fishing. One day I came upon a long deep run on the San Juan. Trout were suspended, easily visible, and actively feeding. Sometimes a fish came up to the surface. Then that same trout would sink down in the water column to take a bug in three feet of water. It appeared the trout were feeding on midge emergers.

I tried a dry and dropper. Then another. After several unsuccessful combinations, I decided to go sub-surface. A strike indicator scared these fish silly. Weight on the line did not work either. They ignored everything that traditionally worked.

Finally I took everything off the line except for two No. 24 midge emergers. I cast upstream and allowed the line to drift naturally. I didn't have a clue where the flies were so I didn't know which of the several fish taking bugs was taking my fly.

One fish in the general area…but not where I thought my fly was…took it and hooked itself. I saw it plain as day but didn't believe my eyes. Of course I did not tighten the line quickly enough. The fish was gone. Still, it taught me something. From then on whenever I saw a fish in the general area take a bug, I lifted the rod gently to set the hook. It was surprising how many of those takes were in fact my fly. It took me an hour to finally figure it out, but I was rewarded with several fish before they stopped feeding.

That evening I tried to puzzle out my experience. The reason why a strike indicator created a problem was obvious, but why didn't the dry and dropper work? My best guess was that the trout were feeding on emergers coming up from the bottom and a dropper attached to a surface fly did not simulate that action.

The reason for no weight was the same. The weight caused the flies to sink while the naturals were rising in the water column. Weightless flies would sink very slowly. Sometimes they would rise with an uplifting current. They behaved more like the naturals.

Since that day I have come across this situation several times in different streams. I have found deep runs, backwaters, and pools with trout actively feeding suspended in the water. If I was successful in these situations, it was usually because I used little or no weight, no strike indicator, and set the hook at the slightest excuse. Sometimes you get in the zone and set the hook just because you sense that a trout had taken the fly even if there is no obvious fish movement. It is amazing how often you will guess right. That is truly being as one with nature.

Being in tune. What a fantastic feeling. Sight fishing forces one to concentrate on the behavior of the fish, not the fly. It forces the fly fisher to be in tune with the rhythm of the river and the feeding pattern of the trout. I love it.

# Chapter 11

## The Float Trip

Float trip. Sounds restful, doesn't it? Well sometimes it is, but frequently it's not. In many western rivers it becomes a full

*Fish on! Jim Othrow and guide Cody. Note strike indicator and long leader.*

day of rapid-fire chaos. I must admit I have a love/hate relationship with such rapid fire days, but I keep coming back, so I guess I like them pretty well.

A float trip is often the most effective way to fish a stretch of big, fast western water. This is especially true of fast, deep rivers like the Roaring Fork in Colorado, the North Platte in Wyoming and the Green in Utah. Sometimes, because of the peculiarities of western water law, it is the only way.

In some western states like Colorado, the land under a river is owned by the adjacent landowner. However, the water is public. So you can float the stream and catch the fish, but you cannot get out and wade unless the land under the water is public. In other states like Montana, it is legal to walk on the bank to the high water mark, so you can get out of the boat to fish a spot. Check with a local fly shop before you float to make sure you know the rules. Don't go on any river unless you know about the water. Rapids and even waterfalls can be around any corner.

## What to Expect

There are as many different types of float trips as there are rivers and seasons. Some sections of a river are slow and lazy, making for a slow drift. Others are rapid and hectic. On most rivers, a day drift will include both slow and fast water. Water that is fast in spring may be slow, or possibly too shallow to float in August.

The basics of a float trip are simple. A boat is used to float down the river. It can be anything, including individual flotation devices such as the pontoon boat. But usually a specially designed drift boat is used. This boat is designed with a place for a rower in the middle and two fishing sites; one at the front, one at the rear. The fly fishers will stand and cast as the boat drifts downstream. Their legs will be locked into specially designed braces to steady them. It is quite comfortable. Power is by oar only, as in most waters motors are not legal. Oar power can be provided by a guide or by a companion with the chore shared in the latter case.

The type of fishing is varied. The most common is dead-drift nymphing. Here a typical nymphing rig with a strike indicator will be cast to likely-looking waters near the boat. The idea is to get a long natural drift. This may require some mending of the line. Usually casts are fairly short and relatively infrequent as the boat drifts through long runs and pools.

Another technique frequently used is to cast a dry and dropper to likely pockets and seams. The boat is positioned for an easy mid-range cast toward the shore or a mid-stream seam or boulder. This technique requires more frequent casts. Again, mending is often required. In fast-flowing water this can be a rapid-fire experience.

The third technique is to drift to a likely-looking spot and beach the boat. Wade fishing is then just like on any other stream.

A day's drift may consist of all of these techniques. While drifting, the fly fishers will nymph or fish the dry and dropper. Periodically they will stop and wade. It can be a great day.

## Drift Boat Equipment

The equipment needed varies but what follows is typical.

The most common drift boat rod is a medium action 5–weight of 8– to 9 feet, the same rod I recommended in Chapter 4. Frequently fly fishers will carry two rods, one rigged for nymphing and one with a dry and dropper. In this way you can switch quickly as conditions change.

Waders are usually worn in the boat. This allows easy entry and exit, even if the boat is not near dry land. Also, getting out to fish a likely-looking spot can be done quickly. I prefer Simms Gortex waders because they are more comfortable to sit in and not too hot. If you prefer wet wading, fine, but just remember that the early and late parts of even a hot, dry summer day can get quite cool for someone just emerging from the water.

Other equipment includes lots of flies—can you ever have too many?— polarized glasses, net, raincoat, hat, bug spray, leaders, flashlight and lunch. A life jacket or other coast guard approved flotation device is required. In some states it must be worn. I feel it is a good idea to wear one in fast water streams. Although it is very unlikely that you will be thrown from the boat, accidents do happen. Waders full of water are like heavy anchors. If you don't believe me, try filling yours when you are near shore *and* with a friend. You will see just how difficult it would be to save yourself.

## Drift Boat Etiquette

Casting with two fly fishers in a boat requires timing and cooperation. The person in front cannot easily see the one in back. Consequently it is the job of the person in back to coordinate their casts so that the two fly lines do not tangle.

The person in front should cast at approximately a 45-degree downstream angle. This gives the rear fly fisher a chance to fish as well. Both should be fishing out of the same side of the boat at about the same angle. Both fly fishers are also responsible for keeping their lines away from the oars. The front angler should pick up their flies before they go past the oars. This gives the back person space to fish and helps prevent tangling with the oars.

The timing of casts to prevent tangles is essential. There is nothing more frustrating than drifting past a prime spot of rising fish with your lines tangled. To prevent this, the person in back watches the person in front cast. Right after the front person casts, the back person casts at about the same angle. The back person waits until the front person picks up and recasts before recasting.

The person in the front has the advantage. He or she has first shot at likely spots. Consequently it is a good idea to switch positions. I like to switch every couple of hours. If the rower is part of the party—not a guide—switch more frequently.

I loved the experience when my friends Burn and Lexi Sundell and I floated the Missouri in Montana. The rowers job is to position the boat so that both fly fishers can fish effectively. I found that pointing the bow downstream and slightly away from shore worked best. Keeping the boat within casting distance of good spots, but not too close, was a mental challenge and sometimes a physical one as well. I also discovered that each fish caught as I rowed was a shared success, my fish as much as Burn's or Lexi's. When Burn or Lexi rowed, they felt the same.

Persons wading or on shore have first rights to the water. Keep well away from them, two casts or more, if possible. If you can't keep that far away, don't fish in their water. Wait until you are well past them.

Other boats fishing a run also have implied rights. If a boat is there first, it is their water. Go on or wait until they have finished with the water. Again, keep well away so as to not ruin their water and do not fish in it as you pass.

I have noticed drift boat etiquette is often poorly honored. Sometimes even experienced professional guides will tromp on others in an effort to get their clients into fish. Fortunately I have never been in a boat with a guide who behaved that way, but I have seen it in others. Not wanting to make a fuss on the

*Drift boat with guide and two fly fishers.*

water, I found out the guide's name and affiliation and then talked to the people who should care after I got off the water. Even if others are rude and inconsiderate, do not reciprocate or yell at them. Water rage is no better than road rage.

## In and Out

By its nature, drifting requires some logistical planning. The boat must be put in at one location and taken out at another. This requires two cars as the distance between is usually several miles. Cottonwood Camp on the Big Horn in Montana has the best arrangement I have found. They offer a pickup and takeout service where you put your boat in at a location (or they put in one of their boats for you). They then drive your vehicle to the takeout location and leave it there for you. If you have one of their boats, you don't even have to take it out. Simply secure it near the ramp and they will get it later. This is the most hassle-free drifting I have found. Others on different rivers offer shuttles, but these may be in their vehicles and only at specific times. In my mind the idea of fishing is to be free of schedules!

Drift boat fishing allows you to fish a lot of water; often water you could not access any other way. It may get you into more remote areas. Multi-day drifts are possible in some western states, Canada and Alaska. In some cases you will not see another person besides your party. Wildlife and birds abound. The scenery can be spectacular. With a little planning and care, such trips can be fantastic. The drift, whether a day or several, is a western fly fishing experience not to be missed.

# Chapter 12

## Those #@%* Midgers

Almost any day on almost any western stream, midges are hatching and trout are feeding on them. They are a main source of food for trout and my main source of frustration. I call them those #@%* midgers.

Midges, or chironomids as they are more formally known, are a group of tiny flies that look like mosquitos with two wings and no tail. Flies tied to imitate them use No. 20 to No. 28 size hooks. Like mayflies, the midge has several forms; larva, pupa, emerging adult, egg-laying adult and dead spinners floating on the surface. It is hard to believe that any trout, let alone a trophy, would pay much attention to such a small bite. But what midges lack in size they more than make up for in numbers and availability.

### The Maddening Midge Hatch

This has happened to me many times. I arrive at a slow run to find the trout actively feeding. The surface is bulging from trout taking bugs, but there is no visible hatch or even worse there are a few caddis or mayflies around. What are the trout feeding on?

I try a fly to match the larger bug with a dry and dropper. No success. Perhaps they are feeding on the emerger form. Again no success. They do not appear to be feeding on the larger fly. They must be on midges.

The bulge suggests that the trout are feeding on bugs caught in the surface film or more likely emergers less than a foot below the surface. So on goes the midge patterns, a Griffith's Gnat with a No. 24 midge emerger as a dropper. This should work...it doesn't. I try different colors; smaller midge dries, two emergers. Nothing works. Finally I get a fish. At last, I think, I have found what they want. A half hour later I have not caught a second fish. They stop feeding or I give up, defeated, and go looking for easier fish to catch.

I hate it. I should be able to figure it out and I try. On many occasions I have spent hours thrashing the water with little success. Over the past several years I have gotten better. I can think of a number of instances when I have been successful; sometimes wildly so. Perhaps these successes are what keep me trying. In any case, for what it is worth, this is what I have learned about midging.

## *Bottom Midging*

Most streams in the west are influenced by dams. Bottom draw dams provide a consistent flow of relatively constant temperature water. Trout love these tailwater areas. Imagine being on water where 16– to 20–inch fish are commonly caught, with bigger specimens available. Then imagine catching them on No. 24 hooks. This is midge fishing at its best.

In most tailwaters trout are actively feeding on midge emergers all day. They are usually feeding on them deep in the water column near the bottom.

The depth of the water the trout are feeding in varies from a foot or so to 8 feet or more. Sometimes they are suspended, but usually they are feeding within a foot or so of the bottom.

The trout often concentrate in gentle current runs and seams at the bottom of riffles. However, they can be feeding in slower water or even in the middle of fast riffles. In shallower water look for the flash of the side of a trout. This flash tells you that the fish is scarfing up midge emergers and larva off the bottom.

To get to these bottom feeders, use a nymph rig. I will start out with a No. 18 Beadhead Brassie as the top fly and a No. 24 Western Midge Emerger (see Chapter 5) as the bottom fly. Make sure this rig gets to the bottom. Your fly should bouncing on the bottom at least once every several casts. Bottom feeding midgers will not usually come up for a fly.

The hook set should be quite gentle, nothing more than a tightening of the line. These small hooks will grab only a little skin usually in the corner of the mouth. Too much pressure on the hook set will pull the hook out of their mouth. Fighting should also be relatively gentle for the same reason. These small hooks will pull out long before you would put enough pressure on a fish to break a 6X tippet.

If this initial offering does not work, try a small larva imitation. I have seldom had to resort to this, but it is sometimes necessary. Also try a smaller fly. Smaller than a No. 24? Yes. These impossibly small No. 26 and No. 28 emergers are sometimes just what is needed.

Trout feeding on midge emergers near the bottom are generally fairly easy to catch. The right size fly fished on the bottom will work most of the time. If you are not having success, it is most likely that you are not near enough to the bottom. Still there are days when nothing you throw at these deep feeding fish works. So be prepared for some frustration mixed with success.

## *Top Water Midging*

I recall a day when I had great top water success with midges. It was on the Green River at Flaming Gorge in Utah. There had been a massive midge hatch in the late afternoon. The fish were up feeding on emergers. I used a No. 16 Parachute Adams with a No. 24 midge emerger. The fish took the emerger with enough consistency that I was pleased. Then the action slowed as the sun got lower. The fish were still active on or near the surface but not many were interested in my emerger any longer.

I stopped fishing to examine what was happening. Noses were poking out of the water and slowly disappearing. A close examination of the surface revealed that the film was liberally sprinkled with spent midges. The fish were sipping on the surface. Time for a different tactic.

I put on a No. 20 Griffith's Gnat above the emerger I had success with earlier. The Gnat imitates a cluster of spent midges. Spotting a nice fish working a scum line, I put the Gnat two feet above it. A nose came out and the Gnat was slowly surrounded by mouth. Waiting to set the hook on these slow sipping takes is one of the hardest things I have had to do. This time my reflexes did not override my mind. Once the fish's head was down I set the hook. A nice 16–inch brown came to net. It was the first of many that evening. As the light faded, the surface of the water could not be seen but fish could still be heard feeding. Surrounded by high canyon walls, there was little light to see by. Casting blindly toward the sound with a short line and setting on the sound of a take produced several more nice browns. Finally I had to quit. I had broken off my fly and couldn't see to tie on a new one. No flashlight, of course (I now have one permanently attached to my vest!) It was truly a great day and I didn't even mind listening to those trout still sipping midges in the dark as I left.

*This brown took a Griffith's Gnat*

The next day I came back to see if the fish were still feeding. There was a fair midge hatch and some fish were taking emergers on occasion. However, the emerger and the Griffith's Gnat were totally ignored.

I would like to say that I solved this new problem but I didn't. Every fly in the box got dunked and I got skunked! That's the way it is with midgers.

Another success story came unexpectedly one day on the San Juan. I was fishing one of the backwater areas and observing several fish midging on the surface. As usual, numerous fly changes yielded little success. Above me I noticed a fly fisher who was getting fish consistently. I walked up and watched him from shore.

He cast down and across the current. This allowed the fly to drift downstream to the rising trout before the line reached it. Perhaps my line was spooking the fish. The fly was a tiny white speck.

After this fly fisher caught a fish, he noticed me watching. He came over, introduced himself as Bob Evans, and pleasantly shared with me his ideas on how to catch these #@%\* midgers. His suggestions were: downstream presentation, 6X tippet, and a No. 24 CDC Midge Emerger fished dry. (See Chapter 5 for pattern.)  He even gave me one of the flies. What a great example of how a fellow fly fisher should share.

Armed with a new technique and a new fly, off I went in search of a rising trout. Shortly I was in position above an actively working fish. If you encounter a fish actively feeding, notice that it will feed in a rhythm. It will rise to a surface or subsurface insect, ingest it and return to its resting place before it will rise again. The idea is to get the fly in front of the fish as it is ready to find its next insect. When I got the fly in front of this fish as it was ready to eat again, it rose slowly and took the midge fly. In my excitement I set the hook too hard and broke the tippet. I reminded myself, belatedly, that in a downstream presentation there is no slack and the set must be gentle so that the tippet is not broken. I had some success with my generic midge dry using the downstream presentation, but it was still frustrating to see all those fish rising and not be able to get most of them.

That night I sat down and tied some of the CDC Midge Emergers. Armed with this new fly, I headed to the same water. The fish were not up. Darn.

Talking to another fly fisher that day I learned that there had been fish rising consistently in the afternoon just below Texas Hole. I gave it a try.

When I arrived several fly fishers were casting to risers but with no success. I found an area that was open and full of rising fish. I picked the one closest to shore. Shortly I was into a nice 16–inch brown. Next I hooked and lost a nice rainbow. This put the fish down near me but they were still rising further out. I worked out a bit and cast across and slightly upstream of a riser. Another nice 18–inch rainbow was only too willing to take my fly.

As I hooked or missed each trout, the others worked out further from shore but continued rising. That afternoon I followed the fish out as far as I could, catching fish as I did. Then I would wade back to shore, warm my feet and wait for them to move in again. I repeated the process several times and caught an amazing number of trout.

Most times I could not even see the CDC Midge Emerger as it floated on the current. However, whenever a fish rose near where I thought my fly was I would set the hook. Sure enough, most times it would be a fish. Thanks to Bob Evans I had a great day fooling those #@%* midgers.

I have tried the CDC Midge Emerger on other occasions and other waters. It has worked some, but has never been blindingly successful as it was that day. Still it is good in enough situations that it has a prominent place in my fly box.

I have not found dry flies that work consistently. I have tried numerous drys without much success. The Griffith's Gnat is one fly I find that has worked under various conditions, usually when there are clusters of midges on the surface. Not that it works all the time, just enough to make it my "go to" fly. My next choice is the CDC Midge Emerger, then the generic midge dry. I have tried numerous other emergers and larva for these surface or near surface feeders. None has been consistently effective. I am still searching. I have not give up on the challenge of those #@%* midgers.

# Chapter 13

# Lakes and Ponds

Streams are fascinating. The current creates holding areas and provides hints that tell you where trout are likely to be feeding. Lakes and ponds have far fewer hints. The broad expanse of flat water does not tell you much about what is underneath it or where the trout are.

I admit that stillwater fishing in not my favorite activity. Yet I have some fond recollections of special stillwater experiences. I love to hike into high mountain lakes. At lower elevations, farm ponds can be a special treat, especially if they are specifically managed for trophy trout. I have had some great days in both. To skip them would be to not enjoy the full western fly fishing experience.

## High Mountain Lakes

The experience of driving—or better yet hiking—into a high mountain lake is a treat. Clean air. Bright skies. Quiet except for the wind in the trees. Fragrant pines and spruce. Snow covered peaks. Elk, deer, sheep, mink and wildflowers abound. You will be engulfed in wild country little changed by man. The experience fills the soul.

But be prepared. Rain and lightning are an almost daily occurrence. Warm dry sunshine can change to cold and wet in minutes. Take rain gear, warm clothes, food, water (twice as much as you think you need) and a good map.

High alpine and subalpine lakes are usually fairly small and have very little vegetation growing in them. The bottom is mostly rock or sand. In subalpine lakes trees may line the shore and some will have fallen into the lake providing a break in the shoreline. In alpine lakes often the only breaks in the shoreline are large boulders. Where are the fish? The answer is that they could be anywhere, but there are places where they may be concentrated.

# Be Prepared

Hiking into the high country is a very pleasurable experience. However, there is an element of danger. Fortunately, it can be virtually eliminated by being prepared.

1. Wear good hiking boots and sensible clothing.

2. Take plenty of water. Dehydration is common in the high country and very debilitating, even potentially life-threatening, so take twice as much as you think you will need. Do not drink local, unfiltered water.

3. Equipment needed for a day hike includes rain gear, bug spray, food, pocket knife, flashlight, sun screen, map, compass, first-aid kit, and extra layers of clothing. Weather can turn nasty quickly and hypothermia can kill.

4. Permits may be required.

5. Let someone know where you are going and when you will be back so if there is a problem they will know where to send help.

6. Don't take risks. A turned ankle is a serious problem five miles from your car.

7. Use only whirling disease-free fishing equipment. Whirling disease has not invaded most high country waters yet.

*High mountain lakes combine beauty with
great fishing.*

### Inlet Streams

When faced with an unknown high mountain lake, the first place to look for a concentration of fish is at the inlet stream or streams. The flowing water brings food, cool water and oxygen into the lake. This attracts the fish.

The stream will have created an alluvial fan where it has dumped rocks and sand into the lake. At some point the current will slow enough to drop most of its silt onto the delta. The fan will spread out and deepen slowly until suddenly it will drop off into deeper water. The current moving over the shallower water will deposit its load of food as it slows while passing over the drop-off. Trout will gather in the deeper water of the drop off and feed actively. Sometimes they will move up onto the fan and even into the stream to feed.

When wading, as you approach an inlet stream, try to maneuver yourself to the side of the flow. Position yourself so that you get a good drift as the current empties into the lake. The best location to cast from is downstream and beside the main current emptying into the lake. Start with a double nymph rig, including a strike indicator. Leader length depends upon the depth of the water, but is usually no more than 6 feet. Even in deeper water, the fish will suspend just below the faster current. They will be 2- to 6-feet down.

Cast to the current and let the flies drift naturally with it. Start where the current blends with the stillwater of the lake. Work up toward the faster water entering the lake. Pay particular attention to the edges of the current.

Fish can be suspended anywhere—or more likely everywhere—there is some current movement. The best spot is just back from the drop-off or even just at the lip. However, fish typically cruise back and forth in the slow current so cover all the water. A good technique is to cast up onto the delta and allow the flies to drift over the edge of the drop-off.

If the lake is too deep to wade into in order to get a good cast from the side, there is another alternative. Stand on the delta at the edge of the stream. Now cast into the current. Allow the current to take the flies out into the lake. Strip out line to allow a natural drift with no drag. Keep some slack at the indicator, but not too much.

This technique will get the flies where you need them but can present some problems. The slack in the line and the upstream set make hooking a fish difficult. You will miss a lot, but the alternative is no fish. Do the best you can.

### Outlet Stream

The next best place to find fish is the outlet where the lake's waters pour into a stream. The subtle current passing through the lake quickens as it shallows on approach to the outlet just as it does in the tailout of a pool in a stream. This faster-lifting current concentrates food from the deeper parts of the lake. Often the outlet itself will be full of logs and other debris. Fish will patrol back and forth at the deeper edge of this cover, snacking as the opportunity arises.

To catch these fish, again use a nymph rig. Rig it deeper, perhaps 8- to 10-feet. Cast out into the lake. Allow the slow current to bring the flies from the deep water up into the shallower water of the outlet. As with the inlet, fish can be cruising around and can be almost anywhere in the area. However, expect a hit as the flies gather speed and lift toward shore. Fish will often be suspended so try different depths.

Another hot spot is the pool or series of pools in the stream just below the lake. This area attracts fish because of the abundance of food. It has the added advantage of allowing a quick escape into the deeper water of the lake if danger lurks. There is often a bit of a ledge or drop-off between the lake and this first pool. Fish will lie just below this break. Often there is a log jam at the outlet. Fish may feed just in front of these logs.

Because of this concentration of fish in the outlet stream, I start fishing in the stream. I work my way up to the lake. Be careful here as some fish may be in quite shallow water on the lake side of the outlet. They are easy to spook.

The same flies that work at the inlet work here. Unless there is an obvious hatch, start with something like a Beadhead Prince with an emerger or a small Pheasant Tail dropper.

### Cruisers

Fish cruise the shore of these high mountain lakes in search of food. This food can be nymphs and/or emerging mayflies, caddis or midges, and there are ants, grasshoppers, and other terrestrials blown into the lake by the frequent high winds encountered.

Fishing to cruisers is often sight fishing. Fish seem to concentrate where the shallow shelf going out from shore drops more or less abruptly into deeper water. However, also look for them in as little as a foot of water, right next to the vegetation or wandering in and out of pockets made by large boulders on or near shore.

Before you cast, study the area. Look for cruising fish. Once you spot one, observe how it moves and how it feeds. These fish are suspended and may move up and down in the water column. After a bit of study, the fish's feeding pattern will begin to emerge. It will usually have a territory. It will cruise along the shore to one end of its territory then reverse itself and move back toward the other end of its range. In the process it may feed on nymphs in the water column and on surface bugs as well.

Now that you understand this fish's pattern, prepare yourself. Select flies that at least generally resemble the trout's food. I like to use an attractor dry like a Coachman Trude or a Parachute Adams. Next attach a dropper fly. I use a fairly long tippet for the dropper (3-feet). The dropper will slowly sink, even if there is no weight to it, once it has broken the surface film. Some flies never do break the surface and stay on top. Select one that will sink at least at a moderate speed.

Now plan ahead. Position yourself so that your cast can intercept the path of your cruiser. Cast well ahead of the fish. In this way the cast will not be cause for alarm. Wait until the fish nears the flies. Now twitch the flies ever so gently, just enough to attract the fish's attention.

If the fish comes up to the surface fly, be prepared for a very leisurely take. The fish knows that the fly is not going anywhere so it has all the time in the world to examine it. Frequent last minute refusals are the norm. Sometimes a little twitch or very slow retrieve will generate a take. Often the fish will take on a glassy surface, but will refuse the same fly when the wind disturbs the water even a little bit. I have no idea why.

If the fish moves toward the now invisible dropper, be patient. Try to watch the fish. A sudden change in direction or a wink of a mouth opening can be a take. The surface fly may or may not move.

Gently set the hook at any excuse. You will be surprised at how frequently the excuse will be a take. If the fish does not take, let the fly sit there until the fish moves on. The pickup will disturb the fish, putting it on its guard or even changing its pattern.

Patience and planning are key. Fly selection is distinctly secondary in all but a few cases. These high mountain trout have a short window between ice-out and ice-up. Food is at a premium. They cannot afford to be selective. I have caught fish on Parachute Adams in the middle of a caddis hatch. If it looks like something to eat, more likely than not, they will jump on it. If you find the fish and they are feeding, you will be successful, but there are days when the fish are nowhere to be found. They are off in the deep somewhere and no amount of casting will dredge them up. Then there are the turns of weather...a hard wind from nowhere or a sudden thunderstorm. Fishing these high mountain lakes can be a real challenge.

The season for us fly fishers is also short. Ice-out varies with the lake and the year, but will generally be in late May to late June. Ice-in can be as early as late September. Hiking can be difficult early and late in the season. The best hiking months are July and August. My favorite time is early to mid-September when the aspen are in color and the elk are starting to bugle. Keep a keen eye out for the weather. If it looks threatening, get out. It is far better to lose a day of fishing than to take the chance of losing your life in an unexpected blizzard or by being struck by lightning. Don't take the chance, just leave. I usually plan to get to the trailhead early so that I can get to the lake and fish before the storms and winds of afternoon arrive.

High mountain lake fishing is not always easy, but it is always rewarding. Just being in the beautiful high country of the mountain west is enough to make the trip worthwhile. A few fish is an extra bonus.

## Ponds

Many ranchers and other property owners in the west have built ponds. Originally these ponds were for stock watering. People learned that they could hold good trout populations. Nowadays many ponds are purposely built for the trout fishing they provide. Anywhere there is a good spring or where cool water can be diverted is a candidate.

These private ponds have gotten to be big business. There are numerous guest ranches and bed and breakfast locations scattered over the west that feature fly fishing for trophy trout in such ponds. Almost every fly shop and guide service offers access to ponds for a fee. Unguided prices range from $20 to as much as $100 per angler per day.

*Rick Covington lands a nice trout at a
purpose-built pond.*

I know, it sounds a bit like trout by the inch...no license required...but it's not. The ponds I have fished are in very natural settings with reeds growing on the bank, geese and birds in abundance plus beautiful scenery. The ponds themselves are very natural with weed beds and lots of caddis and mayfly hatches.

The fish are large and numerous. In some cases they have been placed in the pond as large fish. In other cases they are stocked as young adults and grow over the years into trophy fish. Once in the pond these fish survive only on natural food and most winter over to fight again another year. They revert to the wild fairly quickly. Ponds are typically managed as catch-and-release waters and often the fly fisher has to have a guide—at least for the first day—to prove that they know how to re-lease fish without damage. The owners care about their ponds and treat the fish with respect.

Pond fishing can be really great fun. It is a terrific break from stream fishing and is my first choice when the water is high during spring runoff.

Locating fish in a pond is usually not a problem. They are in the same locations as they are in high lakes. Inlets are always good. Breaks where the shallows fall into deeper water, espe-cially the dam face, work. Edges of weed beds attract fish. Or sight fish if the fish are cruising. Very often some really good fish are right at the edge of the pond.

## Techniques

For some reason one technique works far better in ponds than anywhere else. It is what I try first if there is no obvious hatch.

Using a 5– to 7–weight rod with a floating line, I attach a leader and tippet of about 9–feet. The tippet is 2X. To this is attached an unweighted No. 8 black cactus chenille Woolly Bugger. (See Chapter 5.) Below the Woolly Bugger is a 2–foot length of 4X tippet and a No. 16 beadhead nymph. A split-shot is added above the flies, the weight just enough to get the flies to sink at a moderate rate. A fast sinking fly will just catch the bottom and sink too quickly to look natural. If in doubt, err to the lighter side. A strike indicator is not needed.

Stand on the shore and cast out over the drop-off or weed bed into deeper water. Allow the flies to sink slowly until they are near the bottom. Keep just a little slack in the line as the flies sink and be prepared. Fish are attracted to the fly as it sinks so a take can occur at any time.

Once the flies are near the bottom begin a slow retrieve. The speed of the retrieve should be varied until the best speed is discovered. Often the best speed is painfully slow…a crawl of the flies just above the weeds. Bring the flies in all the way to the edge of the pond and be prepared. I have had many takes just a foot or two from shore.

Takes come in two kinds. The subtle tightening of the line as a fish takes the nymph. This slow retrieve simulates a caddis or damsel crawling to the shore to emerge into an adult. Because you already have a tight line, the hook set consists of a gentle raising of the rod. The fish is on.

The second take is a violent smash of the Woolly Bugger. This can happen at any time, but one of the places trout love to attack Woolly Buggers is just as they come up over the edge of a break into shallow water. Perhaps it is the fear of losing their meal. This violent strike is why you need 2X. A lighter tippet will snap the instant of the hit, leaving you with no flies and a very disappointed expression.

If this combination does not work, try other flies. Ponds have mayflies, caddis, midges, dragonflies (damsels), and various terrestrials so be observant and imaginative.

Some people love to float tube ponds and lakes. It is not my favorite way to fish but in some cases it is necessary. The shoreline in some ponds is shallow and full of soft mud, making it impossible to wade out to the best locations for the fish. Alternatively the shore may be covered in reeds and impossible to cast from. The float tube gets the fly fisher to the fish in these situations.

When there is no obvious areas of activity or when moving from one spot to another, try this. Use my Woolly Bugger rig. Cast a moderate distance and allow the flies to sink. Now *slowly* troll the flies over the weed beds. It can be very effective. I caught fish after fish from 20– to 24–inchers in Douglas Lake on Douglas Lake Ranch in British Columbia, Canada. These beautiful Kamloops rainbows would smash the Woolly Bugger and head for parts unknown. I never saw my backing so much in one trip as I did there. (See Chapter 29.)

Pond fishing, like high mountain lake fishing, has its unique rewards. Don't dismiss it because you think it is too commercial. Give it a try. It might surprise and please you.

## Chapter 14

# Pike On A Fly

I cast to a patch of grass about a foot below the surface. The fly, a large red and white foamhead diver, smacked the surface sending out shock waves. In an instant a fish made a beeline for the fly from 20 feet away pushing a big wake ahead of him. He grabbed the fly with a sideways slash and headed back to his lair. I recovered from the shock and set the hook. Nothing.

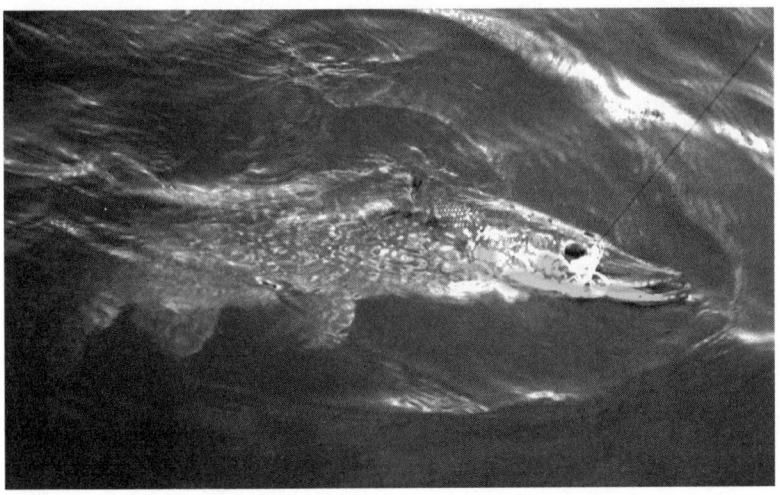

*Watch out...he's going under the boat!*

Retrieving my line, I found a neatly sliced 30 pound mono leader. Lesson number one in pike fishing...use a wire leader!

The fish was a northern pike and I was fishing at Fishing Bear Camp (907–842–5060) in Alaska. What a day. Pike after pike smashed my diver as it struggled on the surface. Some would hit it instantly. Others would follow it and hit a few feet from me as I waded along the shore. Strikes were frequent and violent. Fish attacked from any angle without warning. It was a terrifying and absolutely wonderful afternoon, one I will never forget. I was introduced to this diver fishing for pike by guide

Gregg Friedman out of The Estes Angler, Estes Park, Colorado (970–586–2110).

That was my first experience with pike on a fly, but it certainly wasn't going to be my last. I had caught a lot of pike in Wisconsin in my younger days but using spinning gear. I remembered their attitude fondly. When my friend Hugh Langevin said that he and some friends were going to northern Saskatchewan for trophy pike the next spring, I sort of invited myself along. Earlier that year Hugh had caught a 50–incher. He and the group had caught many pike over 36 inches and many more of somewhat lesser statue. (See Brian McKinley, "Hugh's Big Fish," *Midwest Flyfishing*, 1999.)

I couldn't wait. The trip would be fulfilling a lifetime quest. I arrived seeking lessons in pike fishing on a fly and hoping for a big one—my hope was for one over 40 inches. I got both and fulfilled my dream beyond my wildest expectations.

## *Equipment*

The first lesson was equipment. Most pike fishers recommend a 9– or 10–weight rod. They are necessary even if you are going for small pike. A rod of this size is needed to cast the big wind-resistant flies used to attract the fish. I used a 10–weight in Saskatchewan and it worked great. My 7–weight was a little under-gunned, but acceptable.

Leaders are stout. The butt should be 30–pound mono about 6 feet long. The stiffer materials like Maxima are best as they allow the fly to turn over. Twenty pound is plenty strong enough for the fish but casts like a wet noodle. Believe me. I tried it for three days and was worn out. Observing my problem, Hugh switched me to the stiff 30–pound Maxima and my casting troubles were over.

Below the leader you must attach 12– to 24–inches of wire tippet. This wire will become twisted and kinked by the pike so be prepared to change it frequently. There are many wire leaders on the market but most require special crimping or other operations to tie the wire to the leader and the fly. Only one, American Fishing Wire Surflon-Micro Supreme, can be tied with regular fishing knots. (Available from Cabela's 800–237–4444.) It comes in various strengths from 20–pounds, which is heavy enough, and in clear or camouflage. I used clear but Hugh said that sometimes clear shows up too much so he dyes his brown with Rit dye.

To attach the wire tippet to the leader I used a regular triple surgeon's knot. Hugh prefers an Albright knot and Brian uses a loop-to-loop system, but I had no problems with the simpler surgeon's.

Use a simple figure eight knot to tie on the fly. Brian McKinley discovered this knot and it sure has made life simpler. To tie this knot pass the wire through the eye, make one complete twist around the tippet, and pass the tag end through the loop at the eye. Tighten (it will form a figure eight at the eye as it tightens), making sure it is not slipping...if it does, you put the tag end through the loop in the wrong direction...clip the tag end and you are done. These two knots never failed for any of us, even when the guides grabbed the leader and horsed in a still rambunctious 40–inch northern weighing over 20 pounds.

Flies run from simple to complex. In Saskatchewan we used Deceivers, Whistlers and Bunnyflies. They are all imitations of bait fish, or at least give the general impression of the pike's usual meal. Alternatively these flies attract the pike and bring out its considerable aggression.

The simplest is a Bunnyfly. It is made with two to four strips of rabbit fur and something sparkling. The bright colors and sparkle of Krystal Flash or Flashabou are highly effective and certainly not imitative of bait fish. In my version I used tin dumbbell eyes and a collar of hackle on a 3/0 short shank saltwater hook, with the barb mashed down, of course. Hugh used bead chain eyes on some of his flies so they are lighter. This lighter weight proved useful in very shallow water. In others he uses lead as well as bead chain to get them down faster. It is best to have some of each so you can adjust to the water you are fishing. My favorite color is the red and white that is traditional for Dardevel Spoons. Other colors that worked well are black, black and orange, and yellow and orange.

Deceivers are traditional bucktail and hackle streamers. Again the above plus blue and white are the best colors.

The Whistler was designed by Dan Blanton. (See *American Angler*/March–April 1993, p. 30 for complete tying instructions.)

It is unique in that the design has a red collar which looks like flaring gills when stripped and its forward-weight distribution gives it a jigging action. It is the most complex to tie.

All these flies and colors work. Sometimes the pike are picky. Other times most colors and designs will be effective.

At times, like my day in Alaska, pike will take surface flies. The Diver is a simple surface fly to tie. The head is a cone-shaped foam available at most fly shops. Glue this onto a 3/0 or 2/0 hook with SuperGlue pointing the small end toward the eye and just behind it. After the SuperGlue has set overnight, tie rabbit fur strips and some sparkle in at the bend of the hook. Finally, wrap hen hackle behind the wide part of the foam head and finish with some hand-tied whipfinish knots. I then add strength and durability with a coating of SuperGlue on the wrapping thread. However, be careful not to get the hackle or fur too full of glue as it stiffens them and reduces their action. To make a popper just glue the foam head on with the wide end toward the eye and finish as above.

## *Technique*

The best time to catch pike on a fly is in the spring to early summer when they are in the shallows. They spawn just after ice-out in most lakes and streams. After spawning they go on a feeding rampage in the shallows, staying there until the water warms. In the summer pike hang out in or just above submerged weeds waiting to ambush prey. Most fly fishing for pike is a fairly shallow water affair, usually less than 8 feet, although there are exceptions. Consequently a weighted fly on a floating line works great most of the time. For those rare cases where you need to get deeper, just add a loop-to-loop sink tip.

Cast the fly into shallows or over weedbeds. Allow it to sink near the bottom or weeds, then start a fairly rapid jerk-and-pause strip retrieve. Try various speeds until you find what works that day. Hang on! You never know when a pike will hit or from where.

When using a surface fly or diver the same basic technique is applied. Cast, let it set a moment, then start a jerk and pause retrieve. The pauses can be longer to let the fly sit on the surface for a moment or the retrieve can be steady, allowing the fly to form a wake that attracts the fish. Again…experiment.

When the pike takes the fly, set the hook with a strip set *before* lifting the rod. A strip set is a strong pull of the line with your stripping hand. (See Chapter 8.) Make sure your rod is pointed toward the fish. If you see the fish take, wait a second until it turns before setting. Once good contact is made, slowly raise the rod to about 10 or 11 o'clock and take in the extra line. Pike runs are fast and unexpected so it is best to have them on the reel as soon as possible. Almost inevitably the pike will make at least one more run, most likely under the boat just when you think you have it worn out. You can never relax until they have been landed.

Once landed, a pike presents another problem. Teeth! Their mouths are full of them and they are razor sharp. Most people use jaw spreaders to open the pike's mouth and very long-nosed pliers to back out the de-barbed hook. Even so, expect to get a few nicks from these toothy predators.

## *The Pike Wars*

I was ready. Equipped as Hugh suggested—three boxes of newly tied flies, rain gear, bug spray, Polaroids, hat. We (Hugh Langevin, Brian McKinley, Dick Schultz and I) were heading to Minor Bay Lodge on Wollaston Lake (204–982–9680), a place noted for its trophy pike. We flew from Saskatoon to Points North. What a great name for a *town*…well okay, a hodge-podge of huts and construction equipment near the northern border of Saskatchewan. Then off to the lodge for breakfast and orientation before fishing.

That first day I fished with Dick and guide Kenny Chen (Big Kenny). It was a day of learning but it ended on a great note. Dick cast the heavy flies effortlessly. My casts took a lot of effort and ended in a pile. Still I did catch about 15 pike, including a 38–incher…6 inches longer than I had ever caught before. A couple of days later I learned that my rod was under-lined and my leader was not stiff enough. One step up and I was in great shape.

The highlight of a great first day was shore supper. We met Hugh, Brian and guide Phil Wiebe at Dead Bay. Kenny and Phil cut and fried seasoned potatoes and fresh pike with beans and corn on the side. The fire smelled wonderful mixed with the seasonings and the surrounding pine and spruce trees. The pike and potatoes were outstanding. Brian and I finished every last scrap.

## The Double

The third day I fished with Hugh and Phil. We started at North Indian Village, a bay with an abandoned village nearby. Shortly after arriving I was casting toward shore and got a hit. The fish was near the surface and a big tail splashed as it turned. Big fish! I turned to Hugh to get him to take a couple of pictures of the fight. Just as I did, he set on another big fish. So much for pictures. Phil managed to land Hugh's fish in a cradle, measure it at 42–inches, then land mine, a 44–incher. A true trophy double. I told Hugh that if I didn't catch another fish all week I was a happy camper. He insisted I *would* catch a bigger fish before the week was out.

## The Twitch

Later that day we had another unusual experience. Pike will often follow the fly to the boat. They may stay a foot behind it, just looking. Speed it up and they go faster but still stay a foot away. To induce them to strike, fly fishers will twitch the fly. This sometimes works but often the fish will just lay suspended behind the fly until you have no more line. Lift the fly out of the water and the pike disappears.

We arrived in a small shallow bay. As I got ready to move up to the front casting platform I tossed my fly 5 feet from the boat to get it out of the way. When I got up on the platform, there behind my fly was a good-size pike just looking. I twitched the fly toward the front of the boat. The pike followed. I twitched it around the bow. The pike followed. I twitched it toward the stern, completing a three-quarters turn of the boat. The pike followed. Just as I was about the give up and lift the fly out of the water, the pike's mouth opened, it's gills flared and it grabbed the fly. What I did...if anything...to make that pike take, I have no idea, but I was rewarded with a nice 34–inch fish.

I certainly had not found the secret as several huge pike were about to prove to me. At the edge of the small bay Hugh saw a commotion. Investigating we found some real logs just sitting there in two feet of water. Hugh cast to them. One followed, half-heartedly nipped at his fly and resumed his position. Several casts later with an occasional follow and lots of twitching netted Hugh nothing. He told me to give it a try.

I cast, had follows, and twitched every which way. Nothing! It was maddening. For at least half an hour those pike would follow Hugh's or my fly and just look. There, just a few feet away, was a huge, almost pre-historic monster of well over 40 inches showing every indication it wanted our offerings, but refusing to take. Again and again they refused. That, I think, is one of the main reasons I love pike fishing.

The next couple of days we had great fishing but more frustration as well. One day Kenny took Dick and me to Icehouse Bay. This little bay has an entrance just wide enough for the boat. Inside pike were lying in 5– to 10–feet of water, easily visible, sunning themselves. Whitefish were everywhere so I guess the pike were overfed. We cast every fly we could find to these huge logs. Most ignored them. Some followed. We twitched and twitched with no success. Another fascinating, if somewhat frustrating, experience.

### Better Than Sex

Phil took Hugh and I to Sex Bay the second-to-last day. The name came from someone's assertion that the fishing there was better than sex. With a name like that I had great expectations. We started at the mouth of this long, narrow bay and worked our way along a boggy shoreline. Some sort of yellow water flower, perhaps a hyacinth, was starting to bloom. Songbirds sang in the trees. It was bright with no wind...a perfect day.

We were into fish almost immediately. They were only a foot or two off shore. Hugh or I would cast next to shore and get a hit almost immediately. Some pike would hit nearer the boat but they probably followed from shore. Most were small...by Minor Bay Lodge standards...25– to 30 inches, but Hugh got one over 36–inches. The water didn't seem to be deep enough to hold fish that big. We were enjoying ourselves thoroughly. Then I made my fateful cast.

My red and white Bunnyfly landed in a little indentation, not a foot from shore. One strip and wham! The water boiled as I set the hook with my best strip set. It was obvious this fish was far bigger than those we were getting. She took off for deeper water fast, putting herself on the reel and taking out line at will. Then she dogged for awhile. I made some progress but she was off again.

*Author and guide Phil Wiebe of Minor Bay Lodge with
50–inch pike.*

Finding the deeper water no help, she headed for the shore. We could see her plainly, nose pointing toward the cave I hooked her in. Hugh warned me not to let her get to shore so I snubbed the line and she turned. As she did we got a full side view look at her. She was HUGE!

As she neared the boat she saw it as an opportunity for relief. Under she went. Around the bow I went with my line. Clear. She turned and under she went again. Around the bow went my rod as I scrambled to keep the line clear of the boat and motor.

She was tiring. Another run and I had her next to the boat. Phil got the cradle ready. She saw it and, wanting nothing to do with it, went under the boat again. I brought her around the bow and finally she was in the cradle.

The cradle is a marvelous invention. It consists of two poles with material between them. Placed under the water it makes a little bay with the poles at the surface. The fisher leads the pike, head first, into the bay and the guide lifts and closes the poles. The fish is now enclosed in a sack of material. It immediately quits struggling. The fish can be handled without damage to it or the guide.

Phil lifted her into the boat. It took two hands and a grunt. I knew she was big, but this was incredible. She did not fit across the bottom of the boat cross-wise.

Phil removed the hook. He and Hugh measured her. I couldn't believe my ears. Fifty inches! I had tied Hugh's mark of last year. I knew she was big but not that big. After the mandatory photos, we released her. Disappearing into the dark bottom of Sex Bay, we wished her continued good health and many fine offspring for us to catch in years to come.

It isn't fair. Hugh had fly fished all over Minnesota and Canada for lots of years and at Minor Bay Lodge for five years before catching a 50–inch pike. At the time it was the largest pike caught at the Lodge. A few weeks later Roger Budny caught a 53–incher, the Saskatchewan record catch and release pike, also at the Lodge. Then this year Hugh hosts a pike fly fishing neophyte...me...and watches him catch his fish of a lifetime on his first trip. He took it all in stride, pleased for me. Me? I am forever grateful. Fair? No, but who said fishing was fair?

Pike fishing is addictive. The energy and ferocity of these fish is truly amazing. Their smashing strikes, their maddening habit of following a fly up to the boat and their tough under-the-boat runs are not to be forgotten. Even the little ones are formidable.

Fortunately, these fish are available in many western reservoirs. Pike were introduced to western reservoirs to control the sucker or minnow populations. Unfortunately, they have proven to prefer the trout. Many reservoirs which had trophy trout populations have been devastated by pike either deliberately or inadvertently introduced. In some cases the pike are so serious a problem that you are not allowed to put them back if you catch one. Still, when the pike are there they are great fun to catch.

Pike are found in some western streams as well. The Yampa below Steamboat Springs in Colorado is one such river. A pike of 40–inches was caught recently in the Rio Grande River in New Mexico. So check local waters for this great addition to western fly fishing.

# Chapter 15

# The Care and Feeding of Guides

I have developed many skills while fly fishing. Reading water, wading without getting killed, tying flies, releasing fish unharmed; these are all skills one would expect to master over the years. Still, there is one skill that I have acquired which I never expected to need—the care and feeding of guides.

A good guide is a joy. They will patiently teach you how to cast (or cast better), where to fish, how to present your fly, how to fight a fish. They will position the drift boat just right and even row upstream through heavy current to get another shot at a particularly productive piece of water. They will sometimes make shore lunch and will certainly eat it with you in a spectacular streamside location while sharing stories of past exploits. They will pick you up and drop you off, check your equipment and re-rig if necessary. Launching and trailering their boat is part of the deal. In short, they will make the day easy and enjoyable.

Over the years I have come to appreciate a good guide and to be less tolerant of a poor one. There are a number of things you should expect from your guide. Similarly, they are some things your guide should expect from you. Here are some secrets I have learned about how to locate a good guide and how to get the best from him or her.

A growing number of guides are female. I have never had a female guide. They are usually already booked by female clients. So in further discussion about guides, I will refer to them as "him" as this is my experience. I would be pleased to go out with a female guide. I certainly have fished with very capable female fly fishers, but a female guide is an experience for the future.

## What To Expect From Your Guide

There are number of things you should expect from your guide.

### Knowledge

A guide should have specific, current knowledge of the water you are going to fish. He should know about water conditions and what flies and presentations are most likely to work. He should know where the fish are at various times of the day and at various locations.

Such knowledge requires experience on the water you are going to fish. In an amusing article, Hale Harris notes "…there is no such thing as a first-year guide. No matter how young or uninitiated he may appear, every guide begins with at least three years of experience." (*American Angler*, Jan–Feb 2000.) There are a few old-timers, guides who—though not necessarily old—have been pleasing clients on the same river for 5 years or more. They are treasures to be sought and appreciated. Most guides, however, have been at it far less time. Take heart, most of the young, relatively inexperienced guides are great. Many are quick learners. Over the past couple of years I have had a number of twenty-something guides who were pleasant, helpful, competent and friendly. Truly they love the sport. It gives me great hope for the future.

A guide need not be an excellent fly fisher. Knowing about fly fishing and being able to communicate that knowledge to the client is in no way related to the guide's ability to catch fish. Two of the best guides I have had, people I plan trips to fish with whenever I get a chance, never fish.

How do you find a knowledgeable guide? To be honest it is somewhat of a crap shoot. Not to worry, the odds can be improved. Ask the shop person—or better yet the guide—about their experience as a guide *and* their experience on this water as well as at this shop. You do not have to accept the next guide up on the shop's list. If a guide has been at it in this location for 5 years or more, he must own the place or be doing a good job. Time on the job usually means that the guide has seen most everything the water can dish out and has at least a reasonable chance to figure out what to do when conditions change.

If you have specific requirements such as non-smoking or some technique you need to learn, talk about it now. Ask the prospective guide what has been happening lately. Ask specific questions. Has there been a hatch? What time of day? What kind of water?

What is happening when there is no hatch? Judge the guide's knowledge by how they answer the questions, not by promises of good fishing.

If you call a fly shop to ask how the fishing is, expect one answer…"Great!" Ask specific questions and you will learn much more. Where? When? How caught? How many? How big? These are the questions which will dig out what the fishing is *really* like. Fly shops and outfitters are in the business of selling trips. Even the most honest…and most of them are…tend to a bit of over-enthusiastic exaggeration, unlike you or I, who never, ever claim a 12–inch fish to be a 14–incher. You can't blame them for being enthusiastic. To be on the safe side, discount all claims about 20 percent.

### Personality

A guide should have a calm, pleasant, helpful demeanor and the patience of Job. I *will* make mistakes and I appreciate all expert, pleasant, helpful suggestions on how to correct them. Much of what I have learned about fly fishing has come from guides who have patiently explained…sometimes for the third time…how to accomplish something needed to catch fish. I hate having a guide yell at me because I have not presented a fly just right or set the hook too soon, too late, or too hard. This is supposed to be fun, not life and death. Your guide should not take your mistakes personally.

I welcome help; especially when I ask for it. Some guides, however, either from shyness or insecurity, will not offer helpful suggestions, even when I beg for them. A guide should help, especially when asked. Some encouragement or even praise when I do things right is an added bonus.

I have heard guides berating other guides and/or the guide's clients while drifting down the river. Unless the problem is thoroughly egregious and needs immediate attention, your guide should not be yelling at others. People killing fish in catch-and-release waters requires immediate action and indeed I will participate in correcting the problem. Still, it should be done with gentle but firm discussion, not yelling.

My friend Austin Condon has a way of making the point without undue stress. "You know," he states quietly, "I noticed a game warden just a little ways away heading toward us. You might not want to kill any fish in this catch-and-release water." The party gets the point quickly but without confrontation.

Other problems like another guide horning in on your water should be dealt with by your guide after he has said goodbye to you.

I have had a couple of "over-excited" guides. I love enthusiasm, it's infectious. So is over-excitement. Imagine wading a stream and watching your fly or indicator drift with the current. Everything around you is peaceful. The birds are singing. The air is filled with the smells of the earth. Your fly hesitates for an instant and your guide suddenly yells, "He's got it!" right in your ear. The tranquility is shot, your nerves are shattered, and you jump out of your skin. Oh, by the way, you miss the fish because you are too distracted to set the hook or you set it too hard and break the tippet. Fly fishing is a quiet sport. A gentle "fish on" or "set" suffices. To my mind guides who are racing around looking for fish, talking in a loud, excited voice, and being generally hyper are just not fun to fish with. Asking such a guide to slow down sometimes works. Refusing to speed up to their pace, if you don't want to keep up to it, is quite acceptable. It is, after all, your day.

## Effort

The guide should make an honest effort to make the trip successful. If one approach is not working, he should have another, or several backup plans to go to. If you use the same rig and flies and fish the same type of water the entire trip while getting virtually nothing, the guide is not doing his job. On the other hand, I hate fly switchers. Tying on another fly before you have had the chance to give this one a fair try is a waste of good fishing time.

I recall a guide on the Roaring Fork in Colorado who exemplified effort. We were setting up for a lunch break and I happened to mention that I had never caught a whitefish. The guide, Craig Davis (970–927–3441) said he could take care of that. Re-rigging from a dry and dropper to a nymphing rig, he attached a No. 12 Beadhead Prince Nymph and had me cast to the seam on the edge of a fast run. Instantly I was into a torpedo who took me into my backing. While Craig and my fishing partner munched lunch, I caught several of these great fighters. This was a treat I would not have experienced had the guide not made that special effort of picking up on my comments and doing something about it.

## Attention

The guide is hired to help you and your fishing partner. He should be nearby and available to help if needed, not wandering off for no apparent reason. Sometimes a guide will wish to check out another piece of water. Great. A good guide will tell you what he is doing before leaving, making sure you are okay before he leaves.

Generally a guide should not fish. It is impossible for the guide—with an 18–inch rainbow on *his* line—to pay attention to the client. However, when I am the only client, it is sometimes helpful for the guide to try a different rig or different water. They should explain what they are doing and why. Then, if they find something better they should direct their clients to it, not keep fishing themselves.

The degree of attention needed is dependent upon your abilities and desires. A good guide will see quickly if you do not need to be told to cast to the seam. Or if you prefer not to have him at your elbow every cast.

I was fishing the Frying Pan in Colorado one day with two friends. Both had never fished this type of water before. I had. I wanted them to have a good time so we hired Craig. Three clients is a bit of a stretch for a guide, especially wading a river. I told Craig to pay attention to them and I would more or less look after myself and ask for help if needed. He did a magnificent job, getting them into fish while assisting me as the need arose. We all had a great time; even Craig.

## Equipment

The guide's equipment should be clean and in top condition. There is nothing worse than having the guide hunting for a broken net while you are trying to land the largest rainbow you have had on the end of your line in years!

The guide should check out your equipment and flies before the trip. He will replace a worn or knotted leader and redo the tippet.

Flies are sometimes provided by the guide. More often they are charged to you as they are used, which is fair. Sometimes the guide, or more likely the shop owner, will want you to purchase flies before the trip. This practice bugs me. I frequently end up never using any of the flies selected as the guide will prefer my flies, or his, to those of the shop. I will show the guide my flies and he may accept or reject the selection. If rejected, I go with the guide. I want him to have confidence in the flies being fished.

The guide will ask about your rod or rods and will use them whenever possible. He will also have one or more rods of his own in case yours breaks. In that way he insures that a broken rod does not ruin the trip.

## Time

Most guides, even some I love to go out with, treat this as an 8 hour job (or some other length) and that's it. It doesn't matter if you are in the middle of a great run and catching the fish of your life. When it is time to go, by their watch, they are ready to go. Sometimes there is a good reason like meeting a pickup person. It is best to get time issues settled in advance.

There are a few guides who say they will start when you want and stay out as long as you wish. This always made sense to me. Fly fishing is not a nine to five issue. Roger Rehurek of Cottonwood Camp (406–666–2391) on the Big Horn in Montana suggested a split day on one trip. He said that there was a spinner fall early in the morning he wanted to catch and good streamer action late in the day but midday had been slow. He was right. The spinner fall was great fun and the evening provided exciting results and I enjoyed a long lunch at my motorhome.

These are some of the things a guide should do. When you think about it, this job requires a special type of person. Most fly fishers, myself included, would not last long. I admire the good ones and try to be tolerant of the little things. The guided trip is a cooperative venture and the good guide will do more than his share to make it work. I asked one guide who was an avid fly fisher how he could stand not fishing all day. He said, "You don't understand. I fish every fly with you." That is a great attitude. Adopting it, I have found that "guiding" friends, or friends of friends, has been transferred from a chore to fun.

I catch every fish they do and have just as much fun as if I were catching it myself. Well…almost as much fun.

*A good guide is as happy as the angler about a big fish. Hugh Langevin (left) and guide Phil Wiebe of Minor Bay Lodge.*

## What The Guide Should Expect From You

Yes, you have obligations to the guide. They are simple but adherence to them will make the day go smoother for both of you.

## *Honesty*

Don't try to snow the guide. He will know soon enough if you cannot cast your way out of a paper bag. Give him an honest assessment of your skills. The ability or inability to do something may mean the difference between a great trip and a disaster. If you tell the guide you can cast accurately for 100 feet in a heavy headwind, he may take you to a place where that skill is needed. Don't overrate or underrate your skills. An honest answer will allow the guide to tailor the trip to your abilities, making it a better trip for you.

If you have physical problems, discuss them with the guide before the trip. Food preferences, time constraints, etc. should be settled before the trip when they can be dealt with, not in the field.

## *Courtesy*

The guide is a professional and should be treated with respect. He is not your servant. Treat him as an equal. Offer a helping hand when you can. Lug your own equipment, or at least part of it. Besides courtesy, helping also helps you because it shortens the time needed for certain tasks and leads to more fishing time. Help when it is useful, but don't get in the way.

Don't expect the guide to be a referee. Keep differences with your fishing partner off the water. If your partner needs instruction, let the guide do it. Offer encouragement, but don't interfere.

## *Reasonable Expectations*

I know, you are shelling out a fair bit for this trip. You expect to catch fish and most of the time you will do well with your guide's help. However, there are times when, with no apparent explanation, the trout are absolutely unimpressed with anything you or your guide can think of to present to them. A storm in the high country yesterday can throw the water off-color today and the guide would have no way of knowing it was going to happen. When the fish get lockjaw, don't start pressuring the guide to produce. Believe me, he feels badly that you are not catching fish. Added pressure from you will only make it worse. Discuss the problem to determine his take on the situation and his suggested solution. Then, and only then, you might offer a solution of your own. The guide wants you to succeed but in these difficult circumstances he may jump at your suggestion because it gets him off the hook. "We tried it your way and it still didn't work." There is no problem with this as long as it is not an easy out for the guide.

Remember, this is a partnership and you are in it together until the end of the trip. Make the best of it. If the guide has made every effort to get you into fish, that is all you can expect. There are no guarantees. Being disappointed with the fishing is something you both feel.

### Personal Conduct

You should remain sober at all times on the water. Wait until you are off the water for that beer. Don't offer one to the driver/guide unless you are at your destination; never pressure him to drink with you.

Tolerance for cigarette or cigar smoke varies by guide. The guide should not smoke in your presence unless you give him permission. Likewise, you should not smoke in the boat or in close proximity to the guide. Don't bother asking because the guide will defer to the client, even if it makes him sick.

### Play By The Rules

Have a clear understanding *before* the trip about keeping fish. Don't do something illegal like trespassing on private property. Your guide can get in serious trouble, including possibly losing his license, because of your actions. In all matters of rules, the guide has the final say.

### Tips

If your trip was booked through a shop, the shop gets up to half the fee, so a $300 trip yields the guide $150 to $200. Both the shop and the guide have to pay for equipment, supplies, etc., so this is not all profit. Most shops reward guides for repeat business, so if you ask for a guide by name he will receive a higher proportion of the fee.

It is customary to tip your guide after the trip. Base the tip on how much effort the guide put forth, not how many fish you caught. I have asked guides about how much they get in tips.

The amount varies greatly from trip to trip; however, a good starting point is 10– to 20 percent of the day's guide fee split for two clients. On week-long stays at a lodge, the tip per day is usually a bit lower. I plan on $150 to $200 a week for the guide, assuming that the other person in the boat will tip him too, but have tipped more when I felt it was appropriate.

## How To Find A Guide

The major source for guides is the local fly shop. Outfitters can also be found advertising in the magazines and on the internet. Some outfitter guides are listed in the Orvis affiliations.

To make sure you are getting what you are looking for, plan as far ahead as practical, interview and ask questions at the shop or, better yet, talk to the prospective guide. Discuss what you hope to experience, any special needs, including instruction, and the guide's qualifications. Cover fees, lunch, time, lodging, anything that is relevant to the trip.

Ask about their cancellation policy. Most shops allow you to cancel with prior notice without penalty. If the weather turns bad or the water is blown out, the shop should tell you and offer to cancel without penalty. Most do. Some don't. Understand ahead of time.

Cancellation policy by lodges or outfitters who offer week-long or extended stays is different. Expect to pay half on booking. If you cancel for any reason, you probably will not get your deposit back. Ask. Typically lodges do not cancel because of bad weather or water conditions. You come and they do the best they can for you. Last year I spent a week in howling winds and cold, wet rain in Alaska. The weather was miserable. Still, I caught over 30 silver salmon a day. Cancelling the trip was not an option. The only real issue was whether the weather would break for the flight out, which it did—just barely.

Ask, compare, find others who have used the shop, lodge, or guide, then make your choice. Once made, be prepared to live with it until an adjustment can be made. It is very rare that you will have a bad experience with a guide; most are very good. With a little planning and mutual respect, the guided trip will be a rewarding experience.

# PART II

# *Fly Fishing The West*

I have fished many western waters. Some are world-famous, others are virtually unknown.

Finding new waters to fish and then unraveling their individual mysteries is one of the great joys in western fly fishing. In this section I tell you how I find new waters. Then I discuss selected waters I have fished in each western state. None of this is intended to be a recommendation or a location guide. Rather, I hope to convey the character and possibilities of each place so that you might select wisely. The idea is for you to have the fun of discovering your own special place.

NOTE: THIS SECTION IS NOT INTENDED AS A LOCATION GUIDE. RATHER IT IS A STARTING POINT FOR INVESTIGATING WHERE YOU MIGHT LIKE TO FISH. I AM NOT RECOMMENDING ANY PARTICULAR WATER. INSTEAD, I TELL YOU SOME OF MY EXPERIENCES SO THAT YOU CAN BETTER JUDGE WHERE AND WHEN YOU MIGHT LIKE TO GO.

*John Campbell (right) of The Outdoor Source helped the
author find a special place.*

# Chapter 16

# Your Own Special Place

It started with a TV show. The host was fishing a river in a western state in August. He and his guest were getting nice browns on grasshoppers. At the end of the program the host gave details. I love to explore new locations...the challenge of finding them and figuring out how to catch fish in them. I was ready to go!

## A Special Place

Exploring maps of the area, I discovered a state park on a nice reservoir. The reservoir sounded familiar so I looked it up in a guide book on trout fishing in the state. Sure enough the lake had a good reputation as did the tailwater below it. It was not far from my destination stream and from another stream I fished regularly, so if worse came to worse I could always fall back to these alternatives.

The guide book told me that the main downstream water on the stream I had seen on TV was the type brown trout hold in. It also said the two upstream branches held trout. The left one had native cutthroats and the right one stocked rainbows.

My wife and I arrived at the state park campground in late July. The sights were wonderful. Sitting in our RV we looked out over the lake to beautiful mountains and a gorgeous sunset. We were surrounded by one of the most spectacular wildflower displays one could imagine. What could be better? I was ready for a few days of sampling this new fishery.

Arriving at the stream the next morning I started exploring. Public access points on the main stream were very limited. The water looked nothing like what I had expected and I could only attract one small brown. Not what I had hoped for.

I started seeking additional information. A stop at a general store/restaurant proved useful. I described the show to a local fisherman who did not have a clue about where it might have been filmed, but he did have a suggestion. "Go up the road about a mile and turn left. Park at the Volunteer Fire House and walk across the bridge. Fish upstream. It's private property but nobody minds. Fishing's pretty good." It was...I got several nice browns.

The next day I decided to explore the two upstream branches. I tried the left one first. It was in National Forest land and beside a road, so access was easy and legal. The cutthroats were not big, but plentiful and willing. It was a great morning.

After lunch I tried the right fork. It was in much more open country, the kind of country that makes you believe the west is not crowded. The stream was small and boulder strewn. It looked very promising. In short order I had the first of a dozen or so 12–inch rainbows, probably stocked. If so, they had been in the water for a while because they held in natural lies and were obviously feeding on insects. Their color was natural with the beautiful red of classic wild rainbows. I don't know if there were any wild trout in this stream or not. It didn't matter. These trout behaved as if they were wild. All in all it was a great and interesting day and I did not see another fisher.

As enjoyable as it was, there was one problem with this stream. It was a slow two-hour drive from the camp. I decided to look for other alternatives. I decided to give the tailwater below the lake a try. It was a fascinating place in a canyon. The shoreline was natural with brush, trees and fallen logs. The stream bed had beautiful runs and pools full of brook trout, not big, but very active.

When I arrived the water was alive with rising fish. I could not get my flies tied on fast enough. My second cast attracted a brookie, a brightly-colored 10–incher. Oh boy! I had it made. Well...for the next hour every brookie in that stream continued to feed but ignored all my flies. Finally as the sun grew low in the west, I figured out what worked. It was those #@%* midges again! I should have known that they were taking midge emergers, not the BWO I saw occasionally. I caught several on the emerger and then they suddenly quit. It is as if someone blows a whistle or something. Grumpf! But still it was a great day in a delightful setting.

The next day I sought out another nearby stream. The topo map showed it connecting with the main stream a couple of miles below the lake. The guide book mentioned it only in passing but the fish guide in the topo map listed it as having browns and native cuts. A side road which followed along the stream to a lake meant easy access. Perhaps it was what I was looking for.

I started a little below the dam. It looked to be good water but I could only find one willing brown in two hours of fishing. I decided to try another spot. I had seen several likely-looking ones downstream. The first had a fly fisher, but the second was open. I parked among willows at a great looking bend pool. There were a few mayflies in the air so I used a Parachute Adams that approximated their general size and color with a Pheasant Tail to represent the emerger.

As I cleared the willows I saw a couple of fish rising at the head of the pool. This could be good! I laid the flies just above the closest fish. He splatted the Adams instantly and proceeded to run all over the pool. I was pleased with this 12-inch brown but he did manage to put down all the other fish in the pool.

As I moved up a couple of yards, I noticed a rise under a low tree branch above the pool. A tricky cast but worth a try. I came up short, about two feet out from the overhang. It didn't matter. A good fish moved out from the overhang and gently sipped my Adams. This fish was far bigger than I expected on this small stream. I had him on for a few seconds before he gave me back my flies. What a disappointment. That was easily the fish of the day—probably the fish of the trip—but he was gone, so I continued working upstream slowly. A long run with overhanging vegetation produced a wonderful experience. I caught a 13-inch brown, then a 12-inch cutthroat, then a 15-inch brown. A couple more cutthroats and a 14-inch brown. Then a 16-incher. A couple more cutthroats in the 10- to 12-inch range were produced from a pool under a high bank. Around the corner another run produced a 17-inch brown. This was great fishing but it was coming to an end as the sun dipped below the ridge. Time to quit.

As I walked back to the car I reflected on the experience. I had caught browns in inch increments from 12- to 17-inches (I measured them with the markings on my rod). In between several beautiful native cutthroats were landed. What could be better? Then I thought, wouldn't it be neat if I had caught an 18-incher to complete the run. Arriving at the car I had just enough daylight to try the pool again. As I approached it, I looked up at that first overhang. Sure enough a fish was rising just where that large fish had been earlier. Was this my 18–incher?

I approached cautiously, making that same difficult cast. This time I was a bit closer to the overhang. The trout took the Parachute Adams. A big fish, perhaps the same one I missed earlier. This time the hook held. The brown decided this shallow water was not for him. He headed right toward the pool I was standing next to, just missing a sunken log. He thrashed it out in the deep water of the pool and came to net at my feet.

My 18–incher? No. I just could not stretch it beyond 17½–inches. Still, a great ending to a storybook trip.

Are you ready to go? So am I. I absolutely love discovering and solving the mystery of these new waters.

What could be better than to discover your own special western fly fishing destination. How would you find such a place? One way is to go to the well-known locations. There are many famous waters in the west. See, for example, John Ross, *Trout Unlimited Guide to America's 100 Best Trout Streams* (Falcon Press, 1999). Most of them deserve their reputation, but during the major fly fishing season of July through September, they may be fairly crowded. To get away from the crowds you can plan a trip to these famous places in the off-season. Early spring (pre-runoff) can be a great time. Fall is beautiful and often very productive. Even winter can be fantastic if you plan ahead and dress appropriately. I don't mean to discourage you from the peak season. There is great fishing to be had even with the crowd.

However, it is still fairly easy to find places in the west with great fly fishing and few, if any, other fishers. Some require a bit of effort. A modest hike will cut the crowd significantly, even on crowded rivers. Tributaries to famous rivers and other rivers nearby can be just as good and enjoy much less pressure. The high country is a great place to experience the best of what the west has to offer.

## Tools For The Search

There are numerous sources for information about potential fishing locations.

*A place can be special because of the scenery as well as
the fishing. Fremont River, Utah.*

## Guidebooks

There is at least one fairly current guidebook to fly fishing
every state in the west. These books will give you a general idea
of the type of fishing and seasons. Some are better at providing
specific locations and information. But don't take them as gos-
pel. To have the level of detailed information one might like
requires that the author fish each stream in the book a lot over
the season. In fact, this is an almost impossible task given the
number of streams to be covered in any state. These authors do
their best but the information of necessity must be general and
not always current.

## Articles

The fly fishing magazines offer a number of articles on fly
fishing destinations in the west. I have even authored a few of
them. They can get the heart pumping and the feet itching. What
I have done over the past several years is cut out every western
destination article and file it by state. Then when I think about
visiting a state I review them. The articles give me more information to add to the guidebooks. A listing of these articles is

# Fight The Spread Of Whirling Disease

As fly fishers move from water to water, there is a chance that their equipment can pick up the spores that cause whirling disease and transfer them to new water. To prevent this contamination there are some simple steps that should be taken.

When going from one piece of water to another, treat *all* your equipment to kill off the spores. Drying alone will not do it. The spores can live for years on dry waders. The Whirling Disease Foundation suggests that all equipment be exposed to several hours of ultraviolet light. Sunlight works. However, in order to get all surfaces exposed, it is necessary to set all your equipment out on a clear day and turn it several times to get sun exposure on all surfaces. I find this impractical. Alternatively a 1% chlorine bleach solution can be used. This is potentially damaging to the equipment.

Fortunately there is a better solution. Scott Rod Co. (800–728–7208) has come out with a spray that will kill the spores, not harm your equipment, and will not damage the environment. Called Bright Water, it is sprayed on surfaces and allowed to dry. I make it a practice to spray between all waters, even two waters that are whirling disease positive. I feel that we know so little about the disease that it is possible that spores from one location are more damaging than those from another. Caution is the better option.

Recently L. L. Bean (800–341–4341) came out with a rubber-soled wading boot. The advantage of this sole is that is is easier to clean of whirling disease spores than a felt sole. Another advantage is that the sole does not pick up dirt when walking so it is cleaner and safer when hiking to the water. It also works as well as felt on those slippery rocks.

When treating your waders and boots, do not neglect your net. It, too, can pick up spores.

provided at the end of each state destination chapter that follows. Also, *Fly Fish America* has all its recent national and regional articles on-line at www.flyfishamerica.com.

## Fly Shops and Guide Services

Fly shops, especially those who run guide services, are a wealth of local information. Most of them share it willingly.

***Author nets a nice brown from one of his special places.***

They can tell you about the local water conditions, current bug activity, techniques that work, and the best flies. Local fly shops and/or guide services can be found in the fly fishing magazines and in the book *Black's Fly Fishing* (Red Bank, NJ, various years). I make it a practice to buy a few flies or something else at the shop I have just pumped for information. I feel this encourages them to continue being helpful.

Expect a fly shop to be helpful, but don't expect the people to tell you everything. The same is true of guides. They are often helpful but their livelihood is taking people to their special places. Hiring a guide can be a great way to learn about a new area. If you are going to hire a guide, do it on the first day of your trip to avoid a week of frustration learning on your own what the guide would probably have taught you in that one day.

## Maps

It is amazing how much can be learned from a good topographical map. One company, DeLorme Mapping, produces an Atlas and Gazetteer for every western state.[1] These maps divide each state into sections. Each section map shows all the roads, including dirt as well as some national forest roads, jeep trails and hiking trails. It also shows the streams and lakes with names so you can compare them to other information. State fishing access sites are noted, usually with listings of the types of fish available. It has listings for many campgrounds and symbols for others not listed; usually National Forest sites. Topo detail is general, 1:250,000 scale, so these are not the maps to be used on a hike but they do give you a feel for the topography of the area. All parks and federal lands are shown. The result is a wealth of information to use in planning a trip and invaluable once you are at your chosen destination.

Just as an example, I have randomly opened the Colorado map to page 35. In the northeast corner of the map is Trapper Lake. I have never been there but the map tells me a lot about it…accessible by an unpaved forest route, two public campgrounds, probably unimproved. The lake contains native cutthroats and is managed as a wild trout water. There are three inlet streams and one outlet with numerous other named and unnamed lakes nearly, all in a moderately rugged area of the Flat Tops Wilderness with several available hiking trails around the lake and two nearby waters. All this I learned from the map and listings in the front of the atlas. Sounds like a neat place, doesn't it? I have never been there but just looking at the map makes me want to explore the possibility.

DeLorme has recently come out with all its topo maps on CD/ROM in a special Trout Unlimited edition. It is called *Topo USA: Fly Fishing Edition*. Call DeLorme at 207–846–7000 or look them up at www.delorme.com. After a bit of learning about the program it is possible to find any body of water in the country. It helps to have a general idea of where it is that you want to be, so I use it in conjunction with the regular printed topo maps.

If you are planning to hike into an area, you will need a map with greater detail. Such maps are available through the U.S. Forest Service or Bureau of Land Management offices. Also, Trails Illustrated (800–962–1643) makes a wonderful series of maps in tear-proof plastic that cover national parks and forests as well as some specialty maps. The scale varies somewhat but is in the range of 1:60,000. Trails and waters are well marked.

### Other Sources

There are numerous other sources for information. The best source is probably word-of-mouth. Fly fishing friends will tell you about their special places under a pledge of secrecy, with reciprocity expected.

I have learned of several locations and techniques from the TV shows. Some are pretty good, others pretty bad, but they all offer information on who to contact to fish the area.

State wildlife offices can be a wealth of information. Be patient and keep asking questions. Some state offices or regional offices have written lists of trout waters and/or brochures. Sometimes you just have to find the right person. If you have a hint about a stream but cannot find any information, ask for the name and phone number of the wildlife officer and/or fisheries biologist who supervises that water. They will know it as well as anyone.

Local fly fishers have a wealth of information. Find the local chapters of Trout Unlimited or Federation of Fly Fishers. Call, write, or use the internet. They may be very helpful. Sometimes they will even go to the stream with you. What could be better, a local to show you the ropes? In any case you should be a member of one or both organizations in order to keep up with coldwater fisheries and help preserve this sport.

Then there is the internet. You can find anything on it and that's the problem. Today there are 6000 plus sites that come up when you search "flyfishing" on the web.. Many sites are not useful, but there are gems among them. To find *any* state or provincial fish and wildlife web site call up http://hunts.net/f%26gindex.html. Some sites are more useful than others, but all have something of value. The Trout Unlimited site, www.tu.org, can get you a list of local chapters and much useful information. The FFF site, www.fedflyfishers.org, has a listing of local clubs by state.

Finally the ads in magazines and on-line offer lots of guides, lodges and trips. Quality control can be a problem. I have found that guides/lodges that are listed through a major organization such as Orvis, L. L. Bean, etc. are generally good. They have to be or the organization would drop them. Otherwise, check them out by asking for references and following up.

## Have Fun

The combination of these resources can provide you with a great deal of information. Gather as much as you feel you need. As the trip approaches, contact people again to learn of special circumstances. For example, some authority could have decided yesterday to open the gates to the dam and flood the river. This could be good or bad. At least if you call ahead you will be prepared and can make adjustments if needed.

If you go with the attitude that you are exploring and intend to have fun, you will. Success is not always measured by the number of fish you catch. If you arrive with pre-conceived ideas like "I must catch 50 fish for this to be a success," you are likely to be disappointed. But, if your approach is to have fun, even if you don't catch many fish, you will be more relaxed. As a result you will have fun and may even catch more fish.

[1]     DeLorme Mapping, P O Box 298, Yarmouth, ME 04096, 207–846–7000, www.delorme.com.

# Chapter 17

## *Alaska*

Alaska. Perhaps no other single word can make the juices of a fly fisher flow faster. Big fish…lots of them…easy to catch in pristine unfished (not just uncrowded) waters. Wildlife in abundance.

***Denise Kahler with humpback salmon from Stream X near Juneau.***

A mysteriously quiet native guide. This is the stuff dreams are made of.

Dream it is. I have had days where I could not keep them off the hook, but I've also had days that were tough by any standard. Uncrowded? There are lots of places *if* you take a boat, plane, or hike to get away from the few roads, but they aren't unfished and in some cases fly-ins or other local lodges can make even these seemingly remote placed crowded. Some more easily accessible drive-up sites have been so crowded I barely had space to cast. As for the native guides, most of my guides have been from the lower 48; many work out of fly shops I frequent. None have been Native American.

So it is not the dream, but it can be close *if* you take some time to plan and are willing to spend some money. To get to most of the uncrowded good fishing at a minimum you need a boat and usually a plane. Planes are expensive in Alaska. You also need to know what to expect and where you are. A good guide or outfitter is imperative unless you are very comfortable in true wilderness where help may not be available for days and bears are a constant possibility.

Still, Alaska is a compelling attraction to me. I made my *trip of a lifetime* expecting never to go back. The next year I was back. I couldn't help myself. Then the next year I spent twice as much time at two different lodges. My wife and I are already planning to take our RV up there next year so there will be more time to fish and explore. In short…Alaska is addictive!

## What Do You Want To Catch?

When I first started investigating Alaska I made lots of phone calls. I kept getting the same question, "What do you want to fish for?" It made no real sense to me then. I would respond with something like, "What is good?" The answer, invariably, was "It depends on when you come." Alaska is a state of seasons and these seasons mostly revolve around the salmon.

There are five varieties of salmon; king, sockeye, humpback, chum and silver. Each arrives at different river systems at different time of the summer. Mostly kings (chinook) are early; mid-June into July. Mostly silvers (coho) are late; mid-August into early October. Sockeyes (reds) are mid-summer fish but can be as late as October with more than one run in some rivers. Humpbacks (pinks) come every other year in most rivers. Chum (dog) runs are more spread out over the entire summer.

The other fish that may be available at a particular location are rainbow trout, grayling, steelhead, lake trout, char, Dolly Varden and northern pike. Not all areas have all these fish. Like the salmon, the fishing is best for some of the species at a particular time. Check out timing for each location you may consider. Grayling are the exception, they seem always to be available.

The best thing to do is ask. Most lodges and outfitters have charts which show when the fishing is typically good for any specie. Understand, this is not a guarantee. The fish show up when they feel like it, but the lodge charts are usually accurate.

### What Fish?

Having never caught most of these fish, you probably still don't know what you want to catch. Let me handicap them for you. Now this is only my opinion and may not correspond at all with your preferences, but for what it's worth, here it is.

For me the primary reason to go to Alaska is salmon and other species are a very pleasurable bonus. I have caught all five species of salmon in Alaska under various conditions. One thing I have learned is that you want to fish for them in relatively shallow, clear water. It would be good if this clear water is near the ocean so the fish are fresher, but that is not a major problem. These fish are strong no matter where they are caught.

Perhaps this seems like a strange requirement. However, not all streams in Alaska are clear. Some look like liquid concrete most of the summer. The color comes from glacial silt or flour...rock ground to a very fine powder by the thick ice of glaciers and released as the terminus of the glacier melts. Salmon find their way up these streams and spawn in the clear tributaries. How they can breath in this stuff is a mystery, but they do. People do fish successfully in this liquid concrete. To me it is unappealing.

Many of Alaska's rivers are big, fast, and deep, especially near the ocean. To catch fish in them usually you have to get your fly down near the bottom. This is especially true for kings. To do this requires heavy flies and full sink fly lines. I find this exhausting work, not fun, so I avoid it. Shallower upstream tributaries are a more enjoyable alternative.

### Handicapping Salmon

Of the five salmon there are two contenders for my favorite, kings and silvers. Let's talk about the others first.

Sockeye are the best eating but where you will probably be fishing it will be difficult to bring fish home. Fresh or smoked sockeye are for sale relatively inexpensively all over Alaska. Going there at $2,000 to $6,000 a week to catch fish to eat strikes me as inefficient. Besides which, most salmon runs are stressed by over-harvest so catch-and-release will help these populations recover. At the back of this chapter is a listing for a place that will send you all the fresh or smoked sockeye you might want. It is excellent.

As a sport fish, sockeye are okay. Fresh out of the ocean they are tough and take flies readily. Once a ways up a river system they quit feeding and only take a fly reluctantly. It is fascinating to stand next to 50 or more sockeye and try to get them to take your fly. Nobody really knows why they do, but it is clear that their takes are usually infrequent except in areas where they are fresh out of salt water. I have bounced a fly off the nose of a sockeye repeatedly and never got it to take. Switching flies had no effect, yet the next fish may take the fly on the first presentation.

Thick pods of 6– to 15–pound fish parading upstream or schooling in slow water are a sight never to be forgotten. That primitive urge drives them up rivers and through lakes in large numbers (although much fewer than in past years due primarily to over-harvesting). As they do, they turn red with green heads. The males develop hooked jaws. The sight reaffirms my faith in Mother Earth.

These thick schools, however, present a problem. If you cast into the middle you will get a hookup virtually every time. It is almost impossible to avoid foul hooking one. This is known as the dreaded back or tail bite. I find doing this repeated to be disgusting. To avoid it, I fish to the edge of the school only.

Once hooked in the mouth, a sockeye is a tough contender. The fight consists of runs and bulldogging. They almost never jump. A 7– or 8–weight rod is adequate. Flies are sparsely tied and very colorful. Chartreuse and pink are the best colors.

Chum (dog) salmon were thought of as dog food by early Alaskans, hence the name. Chums are in most river systems and may run continuously from late June into September. As they enter fresh water they change to a green body color with irregular splotches of deep purplish red. This sounds more attractive than it is.

On the other hand, chum take almost any streamer readily. I have even caught them on egg patterns while fishing for char and rainbows. Chum are tough fighters. About the same size as sockeyes, they fight deep. No spectacular runs, just strong resistance. They are an added bonus when fishing for other salmon.

Humpback (pink) salmon are smaller than sockeye or chums. The males become almost grotesque as they enter fresh water. They develop an extended hook jaw that is so pronounced that it does not allow the mouth to close. Add to this a huge hump on the back that can make a fish appear deeper than it is long, and you have a very peculiar looking animal.

I have only fished for pinks once, but what a half-day trip. We flew out of Juneau to "Stream X," not named by the outfitter because he didn't want others to know about it. The float plane landed in the ocean and taxied to shore next to a modest stream. Our guide gave us instructions about bear watching and tied simple streamers on 0X tippet. We were off!

On my first cast I got a hit, shortly landing my first pink. On my second cast I got another. They were thick and easily visible just feet away in the pools 100 yards up from the ocean. On my third cast I caught another. This continued for over two hours. I may have actually missed a fish on a half-dozen different casts. Often if a fish missed the fly, it or another would hit the fly again before it moved a few feet. After a while I decided I would cast and retrieve as badly as possible to see if I could *not* catch fish. It didn't work. If salmon fishing could be too easy, this was it.

I quit and started exploring the mouth of the river for early run silvers. They may have been there but they didn't have a chance. The pinks were on the fly almost before it hit the water. I caught over 36 fish from 3– to 8–pounds in 3½ hours and most of the last 1½ hours I wasn't hardly trying. Believe me, 4 hours of this fishing was enough.

I don't know if this is typical...perhaps not. This outfitter (Bear Creek, 907–789–3914) was really concerned that I keep the location quiet. So no names. I do, however, have the map firmly etched in my brain.

Silver salmon (coho) have the reputation of being great fighters. In most river systems they range from 10–to 20–pounds. They run, jump on occasion and don't give up. They take a fly fairly readily, even surface flies under the right conditions.

One problem with silver fishing is the weather. September is often cold and blustery. I have fished for silvers in 50 mph winds. It didn't bother the fish, but I sure was cold. A 7–weight rod will work but 9– or 10–weight rods are more like it for these feisty fish, especially in the wind.

The greatest thrill to me in fishing silvers is their willingness to take a surface fly. Several articles have been written about pollywogging for silvers (see end of chapter). Pink deerhair bassbugs called Pink Pollywogs attract these fish to the surface where they open large mouths and smash them. A 20–pound silver on a dry fly is a treat not to be missed. As an alterative to the deerhair polywog, on one trip I made up foam bodied "bass" poppers. The body was yellow and I striped it with red magic marker. The tail was pink marabou with Krystal Flash. The silvers loved these flies which my guide, Brad, dubbed the psychedelic popper. Twenty silvers in one windy afternoon in less than two feet of water on a fly I invented created an experience I treasure.

As great as all these salmon are, I have saved my favorite for last. The king salmon (chinook) is the largest of the Alaskan salmon, running from 25 to well over 50 pounds (the record is over 100 pounds). My first encounter with kings was over 1,000 miles upstream from the ocean. Even after all this travel, these salmon were the toughest fighters I have ever encountered in fresh or salt water.

A king would hit a streamer or fuchsia Woolly Bugger fairly softly. A hard set would generate a fast downstream run. A 10–weight rod, 20–pound tippet, and a big Tibor reel with the drag cranked down to the point where I could barely strip line from it, made absolutely no impression on these kings. This is rod butt in the belly…hang on for dear life with both hands…fighting. When they saw shallow water at the bottom of the pool the kings would turn back. Reeling furiously to regain a tight line, I would catch up to the fish shortly after it passed me on its way upstream. After several more runs it would start to come grudgingly to me. Once it got near, the real fun commenced. Shorter powerful runs were punctuated with occasional jumps. Imagine a 35– to 40–pound king…a fish over 40 inches long…jumping clear out of the water not 20 feet away. It is a sight.

***Author with late night king salmon on the Salmon River.***

Once a king is landed and released, the first thing you do is stretch and shake your arms to get the tightness out of the muscles. After landing several I found myself hoping I would not get another hit. I wasn't sure my arms would take it. Never in fresh or salt water have I had such a fight from a fish this size.

### Other Treats

Rainbows are wild and native in some parts of Alaska but not in others. They are found in the more coastal waters. The rainbows I have caught are good fighters and excellent jumpers. If Michael Jordan were a rainbow he would be an Alaskan. I hooked one 20– incher who jumped two feet from me and I had to look up at her.

There are areas where trophy rainbows are prevalent. These are wild fish of 25– to more than 30 inches. People make special trips from all over the world to catch the fall runs out of Lake Iliamna in September. A 32–inch rainbow with an 18½–inch girth is a lot of fish.

Rainbows are fun to catch but in most waters they do not reach these proportions (16– to 20–inches are more common). In my mind, it is not worth going all the way to Alaska for 20– inch rainbows. There are so many less expensive alternatives in the west where wild rainbows can be caught. Still, those trophies are tempting.

Grayling are almost everywhere and they are great. Usually willing to take a dry and not at all fussy, they have filled many a day with action. Grayling are related to whitefish. They fight deep and tough for their relatively small size (an 18–incher is big). Five-weight rods work well. The sail-like dorsal fin and beautiful iridescent blue color make them unusually attractive. Nothing like a pretty, willing fish to buoy your confidence.

Char and the closely related Dolly Varden are mostly bottom feeders. They follow the salmon upriver and feed on escaping eggs. Egg patterns, orange plastic beads, and small streamers work great. A 24-inch char is a lot of fish, even on a 7–weight rod. They are as tough as king salmon but don't jump. If they were as big, they would be awesome. In some places they are.

Of all the Alaska fish, these are the most beautiful, especially as they acquire their fall spawning colors. Deep green sides are punctuated with pink dots as they blend into a rich red belly (think of a spawning brookies, a close cousin). I have willingly given up on sockeyes to go after the char following them on more than one occasion.

Northern pike are available in some Alaskan lakes. I will not go into detail here. (See Chapter 14, Pike On A Fly.) It is enough to say that you have not experienced all there is in freshwater fly rodding until a northern smashes your surface fly! In Alaska a good northern is 30–inches, a trophy is over 40–inches. They come after a fly with authority, speed and a visible wake. I have jumped out of my skin from more than one surprise attack.

Well, there you have it. All these fish are fun to catch. Go for the salmon and enjoy the others as a welcomed bonus.

## *Lodge Or Float*

There are two ways to experience freshwater wilderness fishing in Alaska. One is to fly out to a lodge. The other is to float down a river.

Most lodges can be reached only by plane. Once at the location you may fish the local waters with boats and wading or the lodge may fly you out to various waters each day. Lodge accommodations can range from tents to simple cabins to luxurious main lodges. Food, likewise, can be simple to gourmet. Prices vary accordingly. Most good lodges without fly-out fishing run around $3,000 per week. For this you may or may not get a guide. All flights to the lodge are extra. The truly luxury lodges with gourmet food and fly-out fishing run near $6,000 per week.

The primary advantages of lodges are the accommodations. A roof over your head at night, a shower in the morning, and good meals are appealing. One disadvantage is that you may be limited in fishing scope unless fly-outs are available. Poor current fishing conditions or bad weather can leave you with a tough week. On the other hand, there is usually a good alternative. In most places grayling are available. Rainbows, char and northerns can be good fill-ins for missing salmon. You are not likely to go fishless.

My main problem with lodges is the set schedule. Breakfast at X, then fish until lunch at Y. Fish to dinner at Z. Perhaps fishing after dinner but in many cases nothing is available. In June and July it is light enough to fish from 4 a.m. to midnight. If I am going to go all that way, I want to fish as much as food and sleep requirements allow. Sitting in a lodge swapping stores is not my thing. You may feel differently, so a lodge may be just what you want. If you think you will want to fish after dinner, check to make sure that is possible before booking.

Having said that, one of my best experiences was at a lodge, Fishing Bear Camp (see listing at end of chapter). There was fishing outside the door with huge runs of sockeye, lots of char and some rainbows a short walk away. In this situation, if I wanted to fish after dinner I could just walk to the lake at the inflow or get one of the willing guides to take me out again. It worked out great.

An alternative to the formal lodge is the fly-out cabin. A party is flown to wilderness cabins and left there for a few days or a week. They cook their own meals and fish local waters, usually with boats provided. This is much cheaper than a lodge but requires a party of 4 or more to be economically feasible. There is no guide so it may take you much of the week to figure out where the fish are and how to catch them. If at least one person knows Alaska fishing, or even better has fished this spot before, you have an advantage.

Just because you fly out does not guarantee you will be alone. There may be other cabins or lodges in the area and daily fly-ins are always possible. Check with the outfitter before booking if this would spoil your experience.

I have to admit that the float trip is my preferred option. Floating and fishing down a river all day, then camping on a gravel bar is a true wilderness experience. You know you are in Alaska when you hear a wolf howling in the night and notice huge grizzly bear prints outside your tent in the morning that were not there the night before!

Typically you fly in to some upriver location. Then your party and guides float down the river in inflatable rafts. Each two people will have an umbrella tent and sleeping bags. Washing is available at the stream which is usually spine-numbing cold.

Food is relatively simple-but-delicious and brought in with you. The facilities are behind a nearby bush and are frequented by mosquitos. Everybody wears their favorite scent...eau de deet!

What you lose in creature comforts you gain in closeness to nature and access to a continually changing fishery. Each bend

*Goose landing to take guests out of Fishing Bear Camp.*

leads to new water with unknown potential...to you, the guides know where the fish are likely to be. On my first trip we found kings and grayling the first day (See *Floating Alaska's Salmon River* reference at end of chapter). The next day we added char and chum. The third day we added sockeye. The next we were into one of the jumpingist varieties of wild native rainbows I have ever caught. If variety is the spice of fly fishing, this was it!

At camp we were free to fish all night if we wanted. We could choose what to fish for by where and how we fished. Big streamers at the edge of the current for kings. A deerhair mouse at the log jams for rainbows. Egg patterns bounced on the bottom for char and chums. A break for a 10 p.m. dinner and back at it. What more could one ask for?

True, a float trip is not for everyone. They lack significant creature comforts that we have become accustomed to. But what they lack in comfort they more than make up for in contact with the true Alaskan wilderness. You know you are in Alaska when your guide checks to make sure the rifle is loaded before he lets you go fishing!

Choosing a lodge or outfitter can be a problem...there are literally hundreds available. Which ones are good? Clearly you will need to do some investigation. Here are my recommendations.

1.    The Orvis endorsed lodges and outfitters are carefully screened and quality is reviewed periodically. I have never had a bad experience with one.

2.    Word-of-mouth from friends or fly shops is a great source of info. Ask a lot of questions. Make sure that the experiences are current. I was at a lodge last year that has a great reputation. However, the owner freely told us that the lodge was paid for and our business was no longer important. Needless to say none of our party will return. On the other hand I went to little-known Fishing Bear Camp with people from my local fly shop and had a great time.

3.    Specialty fly fishing booking agents can be very useful. Their business is dependent upon treating their clients right. Make sure they have been in the business for some years and check out references.

4.    Ask the lodge or outfitter for references in your area. Check them out! Ask specific questions about what was good or bad about the people. Also ask the lodge people what the breakdown in type of fishers they have...some only have a few fly fishers and a mixture with spin fishers does not always work out as spin fishers fish the waters differently than fly fishers.

Do not neglect to check things out as completely as you can. Wishing that you knew something after you arrive is too late.

## *Sources of Information*

Here are some sources of information on places to fish, lodges and outfitters in Alaska. It is not comprehensive, but it will get you started on your search. I cannot guarantee that the information is current and accurate as things change all the time. This is intended as a start. Check things out completely for yourself.

### *Guide Books*

Dan Heiner, *Fly-Fishing Alaska's Wild Rivers* (Stackpole Books, . 998).

Rene´ Limeres & Gunnar Pedersen, *Alaska Fishing* (Foghorn Press, 1995).

Tricia Brown (ed), *Alaskan Wilderness*, (Discovery Communications, Inc. 1999).

### *Articles*

Bill Battles, *Cast & Blast Aleutian*, Fly Fish America, (Jan, 2000) p.7.

Cecilia Kleinkauf, *The Grayling Highway, AK*, Northwest Fly Fishing, (Spring 2000) p. 58.

John Randolph, *Tsiu Silvers*, Fly Fish America, (May, 2000) p.70.

Rich Culver, *Southeast Steelhead, AK*, Northwest Fly Fishing, (Summer 2000) p.48.

Don Roberts, *Trout Fishing Where the Wild Things Are*, Flyfishing & Tying Journal, (Winter 2000) p.92.

Thomas R. Pero, *Silver Salmon and Super Spankers*, Wild Steelhead and Trout, (Spring, 1999), p.20.

Ed Engle, *Dryfly Alaska*, Fly Rod & Reel, (Spring, 1999) p.20.

Richard Culver, *Saltwater Kings*, Fly Rod & Reel, (July/August, 1999) p.48.

Paul B. Downing, *Floating Alaska's Salmon River*, Flyfishing & Tying Journal, (Winter 1999) p.44.

Rex Gerlach, *No Crying Over Spilled Rainbows*, Flyfishing (Jan–Feb, 1998) p.18

Tim Jones, *Char Challenge*, Fly Rod & Reel, (January/February, 1998) p.50.

Tony Oswald, *Alaska, Still Wild, Still Wonderful,* <u>Rocky Mountain Streamside,</u> (Expo, 1997), p.5 (Colorado Trout Unlimited).

Scott Richmond, *Alaska a la carte,* <u>Western Fly Fishing,</u> (January–February, 1997) p.62.

Trey Combs, *Alaskan Chum Salmon,* <u>Fly Fisherman</u> (February, 1997) p.40.

Marty Sherman, *Alaska Salmon Fly Fishing,* <u>Western Fly Fishing</u> (January–February, 1996), p.57.

Anthony J. Route, *Kenai Peninsula Possibilities,* <u>Western Fly Fishing,</u> (January–February, 1996) p.50.

Ken Marsh, *Fishing Alaska, A Flying Start,* <u>Western Fly Fishing,</u> (January–February, 1996), p.62.

Anthony J. Route, *George Parks Highway,* <u>Western Fly Fishing,</u> (March–April, 1996) p. 24.

Anthony J. Route, *The Haul Road, Grayling, lake trout and sea-run Dolly Varden are the mainstay of this trip,* <u>Western Fly Fishing,</u> (May/June, 1996) p.63.

Casey Sheahan, *The V-Wakes are Coming,* <u>Western Fly Fishing,</u> (July–October, 1996) p. 42.

## Contacts

***Ouzel Expeditions, Inc.***, P O Box 935, Girdwook, AK 99587, Paul & Sharon Allred, 970–783–2216, 800– 825–8196, FAX 907–783–3220 www.alaska.net/~ouzel. For the float trip of a lifetime, these folks will do it. Great people and great fun in the middle of the Alaska wilderness.

***Fishing Bear Camp***, 400 Ringneck Drive, Kalispell, MT 59901 (winter address) c/o Freshwater Air 907– 842–5060 (summer contact). Justin and Lisa Johns, 406–752–1399, FAX 406–752–1398. Modest, clean and nice lodge and cabins. Salmon and char just out the door, rainbow, grayling and northern pike a short boat ride away, all in the exceptionally beautiful Tikchik Wilderness. Great cook, great guides, great folks add to the pleasure. The plane ride to the camp in a Goose is an additional treat.

## Your Source For Salmon To Eat

***Taku Smokeries***, 550 South Franklin Street, Juneau, AK 99801, 800–582–5122, www.takusmokeries.com

# Chapter 18

# *Arizona*

When one thinks of fly fishing for trout in the west, one of the last places that may come to mind is Arizona. Don't neglect this over-looked state however. There are some serious opportunities available.

## *Lees Ferry*

January brings thoughts of snow in the air and ice on the river, but not in Arizona. True, at Lees Ferry in northern Arizona there is an occasional snow. Mornings can be bitter, but the sun warms things quickly. By afternoon on a typical day you will have caught a number of nice rainbows on midge emergers and will be in your shirt-sleeves casting to risers. It is a great place for winter fishing.

The Glen Canyon Dam at Parker forms Lake Powell. Below the bottom release dam the water flows at a constant cool 54° or so. The lake provides the nutrients and the water quality for great trout habitat along this stretch of the Colorado from the dam to the Navajo Bridge on Highway Alt. 89. There are miles of big water and great rainbow fishing. It has become my traditional first of the year fishing spot...but do not think of it as just a winter spot. It's good all the time.

There are two ways to fish Lees Ferry: taking a boat and guide upstream, or fishing the limited area of the river in the vicinity of the boat ramp.

A boat is required to get to most of the water. What a boat trip. Zipping along in a jet boat on smooth water as the sun tips cliffs of red sandstone up to 1000 feet straight above you makes you almost forget the chill of the early morning air...almost. Think Grand Canyon looking up from the bottom. It's definitely worth the trip.

The fishing is very good and fairly easy. To start you will probably nymph shallow runs. Later in the day there may be a hatch of small mayflies. Some places you wade, others you fish from the boat.

The walk-in fishing is limited in area but not in the number and quality of the fish. The edges of this big, powerful river

159

have riffles and runs that hold fish. Again most fishing is with the two nymph rig. There are occasional hatches, mostly of midges or small blue-wing olives (BWO).

The major problem with the walk-in area is the small space and number of fishers. The combination creates crowding. Personally I would never go to Lees Ferry just for the walk-in fishing, but it is a nice fill-in between boat trips or after your get back at night.

The trout are rainbows that have grown fat and sassy. Seldom have I caught one over 20–inches, but 16– to 18–inchers are common. The State stocks fingerlings and there is some natural reproduction, so there is a big population that acts wild.

Typical flies include small No. 20–24 midge emergers in various colors and eggs in orange or yellow. A No. 18 Parachute in gray usually works for hatches.

Lees Ferry is a beautiful area with great fishing. Plan on hiring a guide as there is no way to get upriver to fish without a boat and the guide who comes with it. (See end of chapter.) There is a nice dry campground there and two motels on A89.

## White Mountains

In the eastern central mountains of Arizona are numerous streams and lakes that hold trout. Rainbows and browns dominate here. However the Apache trout, a rare variety of cutthroat is found here too. These trout are found primarily on the lands of the White Mountain Apache Tribe so a special tribal license is required. Contact: White Mountain Tribal Game & Fish, P O Box 220, Whitewater, AZ 85941, (520) 338–4385.

This area provides some surprisingly good spring-summer-fall fishing in rivers and lakes. At over 7,000 feet, it seems more like Utah than Arizona.

## The Salt River

It's mid-February, I am in Scottsdale for a week, haven't fished for what seems like months, and I'm desperate. So, my friend Austin Condon and I head for the Salt River. The current is slow most places but there are a few areas with runs and pools. The Salt holds bass and suckers all year and stocked trout in the winter.

*Lees Ferry, Arizona. Not only scenic but full of fish.*

We rode out to Phon-D-Sutton Recreation Area in Austin's classic MGA. That alone was worth the trip. We fished for 4 hours, each catching several trout, a couple of bass and suckers on #16 Flash Pheasant Tails.

Not exactly wilderness fishing, but far better than the local bathtub. As I said, I was desperate!

Efforts are under way to secure flows from the dam so that the Salt would hold wild trout all year. The potential is there for wonderful fishing for big trout. I have great hope that the effort will be successful.

## Sources of Information

### Guide Books

Rex Johnson, Jr. *Arizona Trout, A Fly Fishing Guide*, Frank Amato Publications, (1999).

Charles R. Meck and John Rohmer, *Arizona Trout Streams And Their Hatches*, Backcountry Publications, (1998).

### Articles

Kirk Deeter, *Lees Ferry Rainbows*, Fly Fisherman, (May, 1999), p.44.

Charles Meck, *Midwinter Blues & Tricos*, Fly Fisherman, (March, 1998), p.49.

Bob Newman, *Lees Ferry Tailwater Trout*, Fly Fish America, Rocky Mountain Ed. (May/June, 1998), p.24.

### Lees Ferry Guides & Accommodations

*Lees Ferry Anglers* 800–962–9755. An Orvis endorsed fly shop fully stocked with guide service. The guides can be booked, so plan and call ahead.

*Marble Canyon Lodge* 800–726–1789. Clean, simple and convenient on 89A just at the turnoff. A restaurant on site and a convenience store/gas station next door.

# Chapter 19

# California

California is not all beaches and ocean. It is also high mountains dotted with lakes and streams. Trout are found in a wide variety of waters. Salmon, steelhead and sea run cutthroat used to mount massive runs up its coastal rivers. Nowadays these runs are a trickle in a few streams and extinct in others. Commercial interests bent on destroying even these remnants are being met by endangered specie advocates and fishers equally determined to preserve them. There are a few places in northern California where fishing for these sea runs is still possible. I have not explored them yet nor have I extensively fished northern California yet, but I have read enough to have placed a trip there high on my wish list.

## The Little Truckee

The Little Truckee River enters the Truckee on its way east from Lake Tahoe just before it splashes into Nevada near Reno. It is a small tailwater fishery with stocked and wild rainbows and browns. Not notable except for its closeness to my in-laws and one frustrating fish.

The Little Truckee has two impoundments on it. Between them is a couple of miles of shallow meadow tailwater. It is easy to fish and I have been rewarded with a few rainbows and browns each August I fished it.

I always start at a particular parking lot. The trail leads to a run with a large boulder in its middle. As you would expect, the boulder breaks the current, leaving a nice pocket below it. The first thing I do is fish from the bottom of this run up to the pocket. I use a No. 12 Coachman Trude and a Beadhead Brassie, my standard rig. When I get to the pocket I make a careful cast to the best spot. Every trip on the first cast a large fish smashes the Coachman the instant it is in range then proceeds to spit it out before I can set the hook. I miss him—I always miss him. Try another fly. He will not come up to anything else. He won't take a nymph, any nymph I throw at him anyway. Rest him for awhile. No good. He is good for one rise a day and only to the Coachman. I know he is a big brown though I have never seen him. Still, I absolutely love him.

## East Walker River

Searching for other waters near Reno, I came upon a one-page article on the East Walker River. Another tailwater, it empties from the Bridgeport Reservoir east into Nevada. It is reported to be full of big browns.

I arrived to find long runs and deep pools , more meadow stream than tailwater. Two days of fishing produced only small browns. Still, enjoyable fishing.

The second day, as I worked up the river toward one of the few riffles near the dam, I caught a couple of 12–inch browns on the edge of the current. The fly was a No. 16 Beadhead Prince nymph below my No. 12 Royal Coachman Trude. As I got to the head of the riffle there was a small pocket of slow water where the fast water passed some rocks. Perfect spot for a fish!

I cast to the pocket and waited. Shortly the fly disappeared. A fish had taken the Prince. Feeling the hook, a big fish immediately headed down river fast. It was into my backing quickly. There was no hope but to trip and stumble downstream over slippery rocks to catch up. I turned the fish in the slower water of the run below. As I gained line, a huge bronze back was visible below the surface. A monster brown I concluded...as did the fly fisher who was watching me from the bank. He asked if I minded him taking a picture. He collects photos of people with big fish. I was only too pleased.

The fish fought in classic big brown fashion...deep and tough. The runs became shorter and I regained line after each.

Finally the fish was in view. Huge, yes. Brown, no. A big bronze-backed carp came to the surface and finally I netted it. Her tail hung over the net and I needed two hands to lift her. The Prince nymph was nicely embedded in her lip. The observer said it was a shame the fish wasn't a brown and walked away without taking a picture. This tough fighting fish deserved more respect than that!

Was I disappointed she wasn't a big brown? Well, yes and no. She had given me one of the best fights of my fly fishing life and was as pretty in her way as a brown. I carefully removed the fly and gently set her free.

*Moose feeding at the edge of a High Sierra stream.*

## Sources of Information

### Guide Books

Andrew Harris, *Plumas National Forest Trout Fishing Guide*, (Frank Amato Publications, 1999).

Seth Norman, *Flyfisher's Guide to Northern California* (Wilderness Adventures Press, 1997).

Bill Sunderland & Dale Lackey, *California Blue-Ribbon Trout Streams*, (ISBN: 1-57188-110-7).

Ralph Cutter, *Sierra Trout Guide*, (ISBN: 1-878175-02-5).

Steve Beck (ISBN: 1-57188-042-9).

Craig Ballenger, *Shasta's Headwaters: An Angler's Guide to the Upper Sacramento and McCloud Rivers* (ISBN: 1-57188-136-0).

George Burdick, *California's Smith River Steelhead and Salmon*, (ISBN:1-878175-63-7).

Jerome Yesavage, *Desolation Wilderness Fishing Guide*, (ISBN: 1-878175-62-9).

Mark J. Heskett, *Fly Fishing Mammoth*, (ISBN: 1-878175-95-5).

## Articles

Ralph Cutter, *Exploring the Truckee,* Fly Fisherman, (March, 2000) p.48.

Carolyn Z. Shelton, *Northern Sierra Flyfishing Adventures,* Fly Fish America, Pacific Ed., (May, 2000) p.30.

Mark Tompkins, *Calaveras River, CA,* Northwest Fly Fishing, (Spring, 2000) p.32.

Gene Fassi, *Fishing and Flies for the Sacramento Perch,* Flyfishing & Tying Journal, (Spring 2000) p.42.

Ken Hanley, *Iron Gate Reservoir, CA,* Northwest Fly Fishing, (Summer, 2000) p.6.

Chip O'Brien, *Pit River, CA,* Northwest Fly Fishing, (Summer, 2000), p.72.

John Nordstrand, *Eureka Steelhead Rivers,* Fly Fisherman, (July, 2000) p.38.

Mark A. Tompkins, *Backcountry Gold,* Fly Rod & Reel, (Sept/Oct/2000) p.32

Mark A. Tompkins, *Golden Trout Wilderness,* Northwest Fly Fishing, (Fall, 2000) p.6.

Mike Foster, *Northern California/Southern Oregon,* Flyfishing & Tying Journal, (Fall, 2000) p.12.

Bill Sunderland, *There's Gold in Them Hills,* American Angler, (January/February, 1999) p. 51.

Chip O'Brien, *Upper Sacramento River, CA,* Northwestern Flyfishing, (Summer, 1999) p. 40.

Steve Beck, *Backcountry Creeks of Yosemite,* Flyfishing & Tying Journal, (Summer, 1999), p. 19.

Rex Gerlach, *The Lower Sacramento Tailwater,* Fly Fisherman, (September, 1999) p. 27.

Kathy Coatney, *California's Hog Alley,* American Angler, (September/October, 1999), p. 46.

Gary A. Watt, *A Season on the Garcia,* Flyfishing, (Jan–Feb, 1998) p.30.

Conrad Ricketts, *L.A.'s Piru Creek,* Fly Fisherman, (March, 1998) p.82.

Ray Rychnovsky, *A Sensitive Touch for Big Trout,* Flyfishing, (March–April, 1998) p.22.

Bill Sunderland, *Stealth-Fishing California's Upper Owens River,* American Angler, (May/June, 1998), p. 55.

Conrad L. Ricketts, *The City of Angles & Its Wild Trout,* Flyfishing, (May–June, 1998) p.28.

Larry Mehelic, *Wine Country Steelhead*, <u>Western Fly Fishing</u>, (January–February, 1997), p.28.

Chip O'Brien, *The Tributaries of Shasta Lake*, <u>Western Fly Fishing</u>, (March–April, 1997) p.30.

Deke Meyer, *The Sacramento River, California's Finest Trout Water*, <u>Flyfishing</u>, (November–December, 1997) p.34.

Dick Galland, *California's McCloud River*, <u>Fly Fisherman</u>, (December, 1997) p.44.

Ralph Cutter, *California's Top 5 Trout Streams*, <u>Western Fly Fishing</u>, (March–April, 1996) p.53.

Richard Dickerson, *The Return of East Walker River*, <u>Western Fly Fishing</u>, (July–October, 1996), p.57.

Ray Rychnovsky, *California Trout Lodge*, <u>Western Fly Fishing</u>, (July–October, 1996), p. 62.

Dick Galland, *California's Hat Creek*, <u>Fly Fisherman</u>, (Dec, 1996) p.32.

Jim Matthews, *Southern California's Deep Creek*, <u>Trout</u>, (Autumn, 1996) p.49.

Ralph Cutter, *The Ansel Adams Wilderness*, <u>Fly Fisherman</u>, (Dec, 1999) p.37.

Conrad Ricketts, *Sierra Grand Slam*, <u>Fly Fisherman</u>, (Mar, 1999) p.54.

Ralph Cutter, *Searching for Sierra Gold*, <u>Fly Fisherman</u>, (July, 1999) p.54.

Conrad L. Ricketts, *California's Lower Owens River*, <u>Fly Fisherman</u> (Feb, 1998) p.41.

Jim Matthews, *Southern California's Deep Creek*, <u>Trout</u>, (Autumn, 1996). p.49.

*Richard Osmond landing a trout on*
*The Frying Pan River.*

# Chapter 20

# Colorado

My home state is full of great places to fish. So many, in fact, that after years of concerted effort I have only scratched the surface. The state is divided into three land areas...at least in my mind. To the east is the flat land, home of large reservoirs, some with great warm-water fishing. In the middle is the *front range*. This area comprises the east-facing slopes of the Rocky Mountains where streams drain to the Mississippi River. West of the continental divide is considered the west slope. It all drains to the Colorado River eventually.

The rivers of the State are numerous. Some are internationally known and justifiably famous. Others, though less known, are equally good. Colorado is a great place to find your own special spot.

## Colorado River System

The Colorado River has its headwaters in the high western slopes of Rocky Mountain National Park. The beautiful Colorado River cutthroat is the native fish of this area and is still found in some of the high country lakes and streams feeding into the Colorado.

The Colorado in the Park is a small meadow stream filled with willing brook trout along with occasional rainbows, browns and cutts. It is sometimes hard to believe this 20–foot wide stream is the mighty Colorado River. After the river leaves the Park it picks up a fair amount of water quickly. By the time it reaches Hot Sulphur Springs it is a substantial river. From here to Kremmling it is an outstanding river designated as Gold Medal Water. Whirling disease has recently decimated its exceptional rainbow population but it is still full of big browns and some rainbows are holding on. With new understanding of whirling disease a comeback is hoped for. Don't be discouraged, it remains a great fishery.

One spring (June) day I was fishing one of the public access areas. The water was high and a bit off-color so I set up a nymph rig to explore the deeper runs. As I moved upstream there was an area where the water flooded the grass on the edge of the river. The water was knee deep. I cast my nymph rig along this bank to see if any fish were hanging on the edge. To my surprise a hefty brown smashed my orange yarn strike indicator. I laughed and moved a little upstream. Another brown smashed my indicator. Time to pull back and re-assess things.

I searched through my boxes and found a No. 8 orange-bodied Stimulator, the best imitation I had for my yarn indicator. Off went the nymphs and on went the Stimulator. Smash! A feisty 14–inch brown took it not an inch from the grass. This fish was followed in rapid succession by three others of similar size and attitude. Then the public access ran out. I don't know what they thought that Stimulator was...perhaps a stonefly...but I never go near that section without several orange Stimulators in my box and a smile on my face.

At Kremmling the Colorado is joined by the Blue, another Gold Medal River. The Blue is most known for its winter tailwater fishing where you can literally catch fish in the middle of an open shopping mall while Christmas shoppers look on. Some real trophy rainbows have come from this tailwater section.

The Colorado then plunges through some relatively inaccessible canyons. Finally it is joined by the Eagle River, another great fishing river, at Dotsero. From there it is followed by I–70 through Glenwood Canyon, one of the most spectacular stretches of Interstate in the country. The Colorado is joined by the Roaring Fork at Glenwood Springs. Great fishing is available here on the Colorado, up the Roaring Fork, and its world-famous tributary the Frying Pan River.

Outstanding and well-known rivers abound in western Colorado, all eventually draining to the Colorado...many in Utah. The Yampa, the Gunnison, the Taylor, the Animas to name a few are enough to make my mouth water.

## Arkansas River

The east slope has its fair share of great rivers to fish. The South Platte may spring to mind. My favorite, however, is the

Arkansas. I really don't know why. I just have had several great experiences on this river. It can be fished up- or downstream from Salida. There is quite good public access. It is the source for the *Ghost Trout* of Chapter 2 and the inspiration for *Fishing on the Edge*. (See Chapter 9.) The caddis hatch in May (the Mother's Day Hatch) is famous though I have never fished it. All in all, it is just a nice place.

*Roaring River in Rocky Mountain National Park holds greenback cutthroat trout.*

## *Greenbacks*

A glossy-clear lake began to emerge from the pre-dawn mist. A huge mountain towered overhead. Sora rails and frogs greeted the morning. Dimples appeared across the surface of the lake as trout gently rose. I scrambled to get my fly tied on.

After several casts my line twitched. I set the hook on a nice fish. As I got the fish close to the net, its green-bronze back, red sides and orange belly showed brilliantly in the rising sun.

This was a greenback cutthroat trout, the only trout native to the east slope of the Rockies in Colorado. Once thought extinct...and still listed as threatened...it is making a comeback thanks to the efforts of an inter-agency task force headed by Bruce Rosenlund of U.S. Fish and Wildlife, with cooperative efforts by local Trout Unlimited chapters. Now the greenback can be caught in various rivers and lakes in Rocky Mountain National Park and in a few spots in the upper drainage of the Arkansas River.

The water I fished that morning was Lily Lake in Rocky Mountain National Park. It is one of the few places where greenbacks can be caught near a road. Most greenback fishing is a one- to three-hour hike into the high country. What could be better? Beautiful scenery, clean mountain air, wildlife and flowers complement this most spectacular trout. There is nothing like catching-and-releasing a beautiful native in its original wild setting, one almost unchanged by man.

If you go, be prepared. Take plenty of water, stout hiking boots, whirling disease-free equipment, and a map. Or better yet, a guide from the Estes Angler (970–586–2110).

## *Rocky Mountain Angling Club*

In Colorado we are blessed with another fine trout fishing asset, the Rocky Mountain Angling Club (800–524–1814). This club makes agreements with ranch owners and others to allow its members to fish on their private land. Join the club and for a small fee you can fish on one of the properties. Access is limited to members-only and only a few are allowed on each water in a day. The waters are spread throughout the state. There are small meadow creeks, large rivers and farm ponds. Accommodations or camping are available at some locations. Fishing is generally great but it can be difficult because of weather. Don't expect a guaranteed catch. Do expect an uncrowded experience...frequently I am the only one on the water

## Sylvan Dale Ranch

Dotted throughout the west are guest ranches that offer good food and lodging, experience on a true working ranch, and often excellent trout fishing. Sylvan Dale Ranch (970–667–3915) near Loveland, Colorado, is just such a place. Here you will find great food, nice rooms, and classic western buildings in an attractive setting next to a beautiful stream. Fishing is provided in three spring-fed ponds and in the river. Trophy fish abound.

Guide Greg Sheets met me at the ranch. Off we went to the ponds for some fun. This was June and the river was high. The ponds, however, were fishing exceptionally well. We arrived to a glassy surface and no visible hatch. Not to worry, we set up two-fly nymph rigs and settled into float tubes. Quickly we were into fish. Nice 16–inchers were mixed with an occasional trophy over 20–inches. Although stocked as large fish, these rainbows live off the abundant bug life of the ponds and act as if they were wild all their life.

They can be temperamental too. A slight wind came up and they got lockjaw! Trying another pond, we had little more success. That is, until a hatch of mayflies started. Then the pond was covered with risers. Great fun.

The Ranch is a great vacation spot only an hour from Denver. Rocky Mountain National Park is another hour away. There are other good fishing spots nearby. What more could anyone ask for.

## Sources of Information

### Guide Books

Marty Bartholomew, **Flyfisher's Guide To Colorado**, Wilderness Adventures Press, 1998.

Michael D. Shook, **Angling Guide for the Durango Area**, Shook Book Publishing, 1998.

**Colorado Lakes & Reservoirs, Fishing and Boating Guide**, Outdoor Books, 1994.

Todd Hosman, *Fly Fishing Rocky Mountain National Park*, Pruett, 1996.

Chuck Fothergill and Bob Sterling, *The Colorado Angling Guide*, Stream Stalker Publishing, 1989.

## *Articles*

Dave Buchanan, *Winter Tails*, <u>American Angler</u>, (January/February, 2000), p.44.

Bill Edrington, *Rebirth of the Arkansas*, <u>Fly Fisherman</u>, (May, 2000) p.58.

Glenn Bamburg, *Catching Runoff Trout*, <u>American Angler</u>, (May/June, 2000) p.72.

Bob Newman, *Wit's End*, <u>Fly Fish America, Rocky Mountain Edition</u>, (June, 2000) p.32.

Ross Purnell, *Motherwell Ranch*, <u>Fly Fisherman</u>, (July, 2000) p.56.

Philip Hanyok, *Bar ZX Ranch*, <u>Fly Fisherman</u>, (July, 2000) p.56

Allen Thornton, *Top of the Colorado*, <u>American Angler</u>, (Sept/Oct, 2000) p.56.

Deke Meyer, *Caddis Crazies on the Arkansas*, <u>American Angler</u>, March/April 1999, p.58.

Bob Newman, *East of the Divide*, <u>Fly Fish America, Rocky Mountain Edition</u>, (May, 1999) p.26.

Marty Bartholomew, *Colorado's Eagle River Rises Again*, <u>Trout</u>, (Spring, 1999) p.35.

Mark Obmascik, *Gunnison Trout*, <u>Trout</u>, (Spring, 1999) p.16.

Marv Edwards, *Exploring North Park for Trout*, <u>Colorado Outdoors</u>, May/June, 1999, p.20.

Bruce Babbitt, *Catch and Restore (Greenbacks)*, <u>Trout</u>, (Winter, 1999) p.31.

Bill Haggerty, *The Hottest Hot Spots, Tailwater Fisheries*, <u>Colorado Outdoors, Fishing Guide</u>, 1999, p.2.

Beth Parento, *Tailwater Majestic, The Blue Taylor and Frying Pan Rivers*, <u>Flyfishing</u>, (May–June, 1998), p.18.

Chuck McGuire, *Have You Fished the Arkansas Lately?*, <u>Western FlyFishing</u>, January–February 1997, p.56.

Christopher M. Brown, *Seeing Is Believing (Blue River)*, <u>Flyfishing</u>, (Jan–Feb, 1998) p.21.

Craig Martin, *Durango Daydreams*, <u>American Angler</u>, May/June, 1997, p.72.

Ed Engle, *Colorado's North Park*, <u>Fly Fisherman</u>, (July, 1997). P.52.

Chuck McGuire, *Seasons of the Eagle*, <u>Western FlyFishing</u>, January/February, 1996, p.18.

Garrett Vaneklasen, *Conejos Country*, <u>Fly Fisherman</u>, July, 1996, p.38.

Ron Belak, *Colorado's High Lakes*, <u>Fly Fisherman</u>, September, 1996, p.32.

Ed Engle, *Backcountry Cutthroats*, <u>American Angler</u>, September/October, 1996, p.54.

Ann McIntosh, *Colorado's Blue River*, <u>Trout</u>, Winter, 1996, p.42.

Chuck McGuire, *The Cool Upper Colorado*, <u>American Angler</u>, November/December, 1996, p.36.

## *Contacts*

***St. Vrain Angler*** 303–651–6061. The most friendly, helpful people I have found anywhere. Full supplies and guide service to outstanding front range rivers.

***Rocky Mountain Angling Club*** 800–524–1814. Private waters and helpful hints on how to fish them.

***Arkansas River Fly Shop*** 719–539–3474. They will get you into those great Arkansas River fish and some high country greenbacks as well.

***Frying Pan Anglers*** 970–927–3441. Great source for guides on the famous Frying Pan and Roaring Fork Rivers.

***Steamboat Fishing Company*** 970–879–6552. Trout and pike on the Yampa River and other nearby waters. Guide service and people who have the best interest of the fish always in mind.

***Let It Fly*** 970–264–3189. Mark Miller is exceptionally helpful in getting you into fish in the Pagosa Springs area. A nice spot with a great hot springs and lots of good fishing.

*Combining beauty and great fishing, the South Fork is justly famous.*

# Chapter 21

# *Idaho*

Some people contend that Idaho has the best fly fishing in the West. I can't say that I entirely agree but the opportunities are numerous and the fish plentiful. Some fish are easy; some are tough; some are small; some are large. There are rivers with miles of public access, easy wading and relatively few anglers. Just one of these rivers could keep a dedicated fly fisher happy all summer.

The most famous water in Idaho is the Henry's Fork of the Snake. A big spring creek, it is reputed to be as tough as the Montana spring creeks and is just as popular. The South Fork of the Snake is equally popular. Beyond those famous spots fishing pressure drops significantly and even on these popular streams there is plenty of room to fish.

## *South Fork*

As the Snake flows out of Jackson Hole, Wyoming, it turns west into Palisades Reservoir at the Idaho border. Below the dam it is known as the South Fork until it joins with the Henry's Fork near Menan Butte above Idaho Falls. There are numerous access points and great floats. Dry fly and dropper fishing is the ticket in the summer months.

I floated the South Fork at Swan Valley with Guide Ryan Peterson. He started me out with a Chernobyl Ant and a Prince Nymph. This combination proved successful and frustrating. Good fish would come up slowly to this large foam ant, take it and head back down. Trying as hard as I could, I could not hook them. Ryan said to wait longer. I couldn't wait any longer. Still I was seeing the fish and getting trout and whitefish on the Prince so it was a good morning.

At lunch we pulled to shore at the edge of a riffle. As we ate in the boat, we noticed a scum line with several fish sipping spinners. It was fascinating. These fish were working not 10 feet from us. They would come up and sip a cluster or two from the film then go down. Each rainbow would work its way up the scum line a few feet, then drop back, rest and repositing itself for another feeding run. Ryan and I were mesmerized.

After 20 minutes of this I couldn't stand it any more. I put on a Parachute Adams and a spinner as a dropper. I almost could not cast—they were so close—but they did not spook. One took the Adams on the first drift, a nice 12–inch rainbow. After the water settled the fish were back feeding. Two casts and I was into another fat rainbow, this one a bit larger. Then the wind came up, blew the scum line away and the fish disappeared.

In the afternoon we found a number of cutthroats and rainbows actively feeding in a riffle. They appeared to be feeding on emergers. We tried everything in Ryan's box but they ignored our offers. Finally I suggested my Western Midge Emerger. (See Chapter 5.) On the first cast a nice 16–inch cut took it. We had the secret. Well not exactly. Fifteen minutes later all those fish were still feeding and none wanted the emerger.

In addition to the great fishing and scenery that day, we had a bald eagle treat. A pair of adults had two young out of the nest and roosting in big cottonwood trees lining the bank. One adult dropped down to the river and caught a trout. The instant the youngsters saw that their parent was successful, they started a loud keening, the eagle equivalent to "feed me, feed, me." I stopped fishing, enthralled by the interplay between adults and young who were flying and as big as their parents, but obviously not quite ready to be on their own. All in all, a great day, the kind that makes fly fishing so special.

## *Fastest Fish In The West?*

I cast my dry and dropper over a smooth fast run. A trout rose through two feet of water, took the dry, spit it out and headed to the bottom so fast I did not have time to lift my rod before it was settled back on the bottom. This had happened to me time after time that day. I was fishing the St. Joe River in northern Idaho. What a day. I caught over 20 native west slope cutthroats but missed at least three times as many. They would splat the dry and disappear before I could set the hook. Tom

*St. Joe River, home of the fastest trout in the west.*

Loder of Panhandle Outfitters would tell me to set the hook faster. I couldn't set it any faster. I tried but I couldn't. The day before I had found a stretch on the North Couer d'Alene River that was also full of these west slope cuts. I missed a few but hooked about 80 percent of the dry takes. I wondered out loud if the fish were really taking the fly on the St. Joe, but Tom assured me they were. He also assured me—in the best guide tradition—that I wasn't incompetent and that everybody had the same problem.

We had started out at a spot along the bank with a nice small run below a riffle. At the bottom of the run a fish splatted my dry, but I missed it and it would not take that fly again. Several other dries later it took, I stung it, but it got off quickly. At the top of the run were two currents which joined. A nice fish rose to my dry but refused it. No amount of effort could get it to come up again, so Tom suggested we rest it while we walked down to another spot. In this spot I was embarrassed by numerous hit and run artists.

On the way back to the car we tried the top fish in the run again. I had learned the tricky current. Positioning myself just so, I made a good cast. The float was perfect. The same trout rose and took the fly. This time I hooked him, landing a beautiful 14–incher. As far as I was concerned, the day was a success at this point.

The northern Idaho area is spectacularly beautiful. The streams are numerous and the fish plentiful. It is a great spot to spend a few days or, as Tom is doing, the rest of your life.

## *Sources of Information*

### *Guide Books*

John Shewey, **Idaho Blue Ribbon Fly Fishing Guide**, (ISBN: 1-57188-135-2)

Bruce Staples, **Snake River Country: Flies and Waters**, (ISBN: 1-878175-08-4)

Ken Retallic and Rocky Barker, **Flyfisher's Guide to Idaho**, (Wilderness Adventures Press, 1996)

### *Articles*

Dennis G. Bitton, *Big Lost River*, <u>Fly Fish America: Rocky Mountain Edition</u>, (Feb, 2000) p.26.

Mike Lawson, *Idaho's Henry's Fork Rebound*, <u>Fly Fisherman</u>, (March, 2000), p.36.

Daniel Lamoreux, *Palisades Creek, ID*, <u>Northwest Fly Fishing</u>, (Spring, 2000) p.64.

John Shewey, *North Fork Coeur d'Alene River*, <u>Northwest Fly Fishing</u>, (Spring, 2000) p.6.

David L. Taylor, *Kelly Creek*, <u>Fly Fisherman</u>, (May, 2000) p.52.

Greg Thomas, *White Cloud Lakes*, <u>Northwest Fly Fishing</u>, (Summer, 2000) p.7.

James Nelson, *Teton River, ID*, <u>Northwest Fly Fishing</u>, (Summer, 2000) p.58.

Terry Sheely, *Catch-and-Kill Salvation (Lake Pend Oreille)*, <u>Northwest Fly Fishing</u>, (Fall, 2000) p.24.

Kirk Bogart, *The Big Lost River*, <u>Northwest Fly Fishing</u>, (Fall, 2000) p.6.

Ken Morrish, *Middle Fork of the Salmon River, ID*, <u>Northwest Fly Fishing</u> (Summer, 1999) p.35.

Rene Harrop, *Encounter on the Flat (Henry's Fork)*, <u>Fly Fisherman</u>, (March, 1998) p.70.

Marte & Don Muelrath, *The Other Fork of the Snake*, <u>Flyfishing</u>, (May–June, 1998) p.22.

Jim & Carolyn Z. Shelton, *Backcountry Horsepack, Idaho's Sawtooth Mountains*, <u>Fly Fish America</u>, (May/June, 1998) p.18.

Greg Thomas, *Idaho's Silver Creek Region*, <u>Fly Fisherman</u> (July, 1998) p.52.

Kelly Rudd, *Bad News For South Fork Cutthroat*, <u>Flyfishing</u>, (July–Oct, 1998) p.22.

Kathy Coatney, *River Of Plenty, the Cochsa*, <u>Flyfishing</u>, (July/Aug, 1997) p.57.

Joe Evancho, *Idaho's Silver Creek*, <u>Fly Rod & Reel</u> (July/Aug, 1997), p.46.

John Shewey, *A Sawtooth Adventure,* <u>Western Fly Fishing</u>, (May/June, 1996) p.58.

John Shewey, *Lower Owyhee River*, <u>Western Fly Fishing</u> (July/Oct, 1996) p.66.

Bruce Staples, *A River In Rehab, Idaho's Blackfoot River*, <u>Western Fly Fishing</u> (July/Oct, 1996) p.26.

## Contacts

***Panhandle Outfitters*** 888–300–4868. Tom is a great guy who loves this area. He sets up a tent camp in the mountains for the summer so clients can stay near the fishing. Or, if your prefer, he will pick you up wherever you are. You will have a great time.

*Burn Sundell on the Missouri River.*

# Chapter 22

# Montana

Big sky country. Big water country too. Montana is synonymous with trout fishing. There are more nationally and internationally famous rivers in southwestern Montana than anywhere else in the west. Big rivers like the Yellowstone, the Gallatin, the Big Hole and the Madison. A little way north are other famous big waters; the Bitterroot, Rock Creek, Blackfoot, Clark Fork and the Missouri. Then there are the famous spring creeks of Paradise Valley; Nelson's, Depuy's and Armstrong. Add the numerous smaller rivers and the northwestern waters and the high country and the opportunities are mind boggling.

Expect a lot of opportunities in Montana…opportunities for lots of fish and for big fish…but not for easy fish. Fishing pressure is high even with all this water, especially on the more famous waters and in the popular months of July and August. Still there is plenty of water and a little planning can get you into almost any type of fishing you wish.

## Big Waters

When I think of Montana I think of the big rivers. These rivers can be fished successfully from shore at spots. Private property, however, is sacred in Montana and most land adjacent to the best water is privately owned. Access for wading can be a problem although it is legal if you are in the water or on the land below the high watermark, even though the land is private.

Water law allows the use of drift boats which are the most popular way to fish these big waters. You can drift the river, stopping to wade at the good spots. To make it easier, the state has built convenient takeout spots at regular intervals on most big waters. All you need is a drift boat and two cars…one to put the boat in, the other to take it out 5 or 10 miles downstream.

Organizing a drift can be a hassle, especially if you are used to fishing alone, as I am. Enter the guide. This wonderful person, assuming he is good, takes you down the river in his boat

*183*

and has a car waiting at the other end. Add to this his local knowledge and the fact that he rows all day...he's a real blessing on these big rivers. Short of a friend with a boat, he is your best bet for fishing the big rivers.

Speaking of big rivers brings me to the Madison. A lot has been written about the problem of whirling disease and the die-off of rainbows in the Madison. Little has been written about the outstanding browns still available. Don't neglect it when you plan a trip. Contact Burn Sundell (406–682–5243).

The Yellowstone, downstream from the park (it flows north), is another big water with a great reputation. Like most big waters in Montana, it is commonly fished from a boat. In addition, there are numerous access points where one can walk along the shore and fish effectively. Gravel bars and runs are numerous. I spent three days without even scratching the surface of opportunities. The area just in and a little below Yellowstone National Park provided some excellent fishing while more downstream (north) toward Livingston there are a number of

*Ron Hildebrand and Keith Keenan admire a*
*rainbow from the Big Horn.*

access points at bridges that provide more good fishing opportunities.

Further east is another great river, the Bighorn. Crowded, yes, but also full of fish. I have had some of my best fishing days on this river. Call the Cottonwood Camp (406–666–2391) and they will provide accommodations, a guide, if desired, or a boat with pickup and a shuttle for your car. Fish down the river and leave the boat at the takeout. Your car is there and they pick up the boat. What a great service.

I have had some wonderful fishing on Montana's big waters. One day Burn and Lexi Sundell took me floating down the Missouri. It was fall and time for stripping streamers. We had never been on this part of the river so everything was new. Still there were so many fish in the shoreline structure that we were kept busy with rainbows and browns to 18–inches. The beauty of it was the complete lack of other fishers! Burn is now guiding, so give him a call.

## Small Streams

This is a relative term, some are smaller than others, but there are lots of them. On our way to Yellowstone on the Beartooth Highway (a spectacular drive) we stopped at Red Lodge overnight. The campground was on Rock Creek. The owner said the fishing was good, so after dinner I went out for a couple of hours. My standard Coachman Trude and Beadhead Brassie produced a number of nice 10– to 14–inch rainbows. Nobody has written an article about this small stream but it was as good a fishing experience as any I had in Montana on that trip.

The Gallatin River has been made famous as the stream where they filmed *A River Runs Through It*, although several others claim that same honor. It is clear and cold. It also has many miles of public access. Since it drains to the north out of the park at West Yellowstone, it is also quite popular in the summer. There is plenty of good fishing then. Just avoid the rafters and find a spot where there are no other fly fishers. All the water is productive. In the fall this crystal clear water is virtually deserted.

The canyon area is fast water as the movie showed but there is slower water most everywhere else. Up in Yellowstone National Park it is a small, meandering meadow stream. There is every type of water you might like to fish in this stream, surely enough to keep anyone busy for a couple of weeks without fishing the same water twice.

## Lodges and Ranches

Open any fly fishing magazine and you will be impressed with the number of lodges and ranches in Montana which advertise. All promise great fishing and great accommodations. Most deliver, but check them out before signing up. The prices can be high but consider this...most furnish a guide each day. Hired from a fly shop, that would run approximately $2,100 per week, or if you share with a friend $1,050 per week. Food is often included. You have to eat anyway, so add $350 for modest fare or $700 for great food at local restaurants if on your own. Now add accommodations, another $350 to $700 per week or $175 to $350 per person if shared. Thus, an independent trip could cost from $1,575 to $3,500 per person per week. The lodge or ranch at $2,500 to $4,000 per week per person doesn't seem so bad in that context. Add to that the local knowledge and no hassle arrangements and the lodge may be a bargain. Sure, you can skip the guide, camp out, and eat cheap, but that is a different trip all together, isn't it?

## Sources of Information

### Guide Books

Chuck Fothergill and Bob Sterling, *The Montana Angling Guide* (Stream Stalker Publishing, 1988).

Greg Thomas, *Flyfisher's Guide to Montana*, (Wilderness Adventures Press, 1997).

### Articles

Greg Thomas, *Blackfoot Reservation Lakes*, <u>Fly Fisherman</u>, (February, 2000), p.48.

Greg Thomas, *The Lower Madison*, <u>Northwest Fly Fishing</u>, (Spring, 2000), p.6.

John Byorth, *Big Sky on the Cheap*, <u>American Angler</u>, (March/April, 2000) p.50.

Paul Guernsey, *"Bonefishing" On Helgen Lake*, <u>Fly Rod & Reel</u>, (May/June, 2000), p.59.

Greg Thomas, *Gold Creek Ponds,* Northwest Fly Fishing, (Summer, 2000), p.10.

Greg Thomas, *Georgetown Lakes,* Northwest Fly Fishing, (Summer, 2000), p.14.

Paolo Marchesi, *Gallatin River, MT,* Northwest Fly Fishing, (Fall, 2000), p.66.

Ed Lawrence, *Boulder River,* Northwest Fly Fishing, (Fall, 2000), p.10.

Greg Thomas, *Montana's Gallatin River,* Trout, (Winter, 2000), p.27.

Matthew Handy, *The Forgotten Madison,* Fly Fisherman, (February, 1999), p.40.

Greg Thomas, *Clark Fork Hatches,* Fly Fisherman, (March, 1999), p.48.

Hale Harris, *The Bighorn Today,* Fly Fisherman, (March, 1999), p.18.

Jeff Hull, *That Damn Bitterroot,* Fly Rod & Reel, (March/April), 1999, p.47.

Don Roberts, *Trout in the Clouds,* Flyfishing & Tying Journal, (Summer 1999), p.88.

E. Neale Streeks, *The Smith River,* Fly Fisherman, (July, 1999), p.33

Michael Fong, *Missouri River, MT,* Northwest Fly Fishing, (Fall, 1999), p.60.

Bennett J. Mintz, *The Other Side of Montana Rivers,* Fly Fish America, Rocky Mountain Edition, (September, 1999), p.18.

Deanna Lee Birkholm, *Drifting The Bitterroot,* Flyfishing, (March–April, 1998), p.8.

E. Donnall Thomas, Jr. *Indian Summer,* Fly Rod & Reel, (November/December, 1998), p.40.

Chris Dawson, *Rambling Through The Rockies,* Fly Rod & Reel, (January/February, 1998), p.54.

Gary LaFontaine, *The Bighorn River: As You Like It,* Trout, (Spring, 1998), p.59.

E. Donnell Thomas, Jr., *Paradise Found,* American Angler, (May/June, 1998), p.50.

James H. Nelson, *Springtime Rainbows on the Blackfeet Reservation,* American Angler, (January/February, 1997), p.46.

John Holt, *Spring Browns on the Bighorn,* Western Fly Fishing, (March–April, 1997), p.60.

John Holt, *A Stream Sampler,* Flyfishing, (May–June, 1997), p.46.

Paul Guernsey, *A Huck Finn Fantasy: Floating Montana's Smith River*, <u>Fly Rod & Reel</u>, (May/June, 1997), p.52.

Deke Meyer, *Vagabonding for Roadside Trout*, <u>Flyfishing</u>, (May–June, 1997), p.62.

Jim & Carolyn Z. Shelton, *Undiscovered Kootenai Country*, <u>Flyfishing</u>, (May–June, 1997), p.51.

Don Roberts, *Valley of Five Rivers*, <u>Fly Fisherman</u>, (July, 1997) p.42.

Bob Krumm, *Beating the Crowds on the Bighorn*, <u>American Angler</u>, (July/August, 1997), p.34.

Steve Probasco, *Fishing the Blackfeet Reservation*, <u>Flyfishing</u>, (July–October, 1997), p.27.

Todd Tanner, *Casting On The Kootenai*, <u>Fly Rod & Reel</u>, (November/December, 1997), p.46.

Deke Meyer, *Heaven On Earth Ranch*, <u>Western Fly Fishing</u>, (May–June, 1996), p.34.

## Contacts

**Cottonwood Camp** 406–666–2391. One of the most helpful camps I have ever come in contact with. Supplies and guides on the Big Horn. Reminds me of those old style fishing camps in northern Wisconsin.

**Burn Sundell** 406–682–5243. Burn is a big, quiet guy. He is a great fly fisher and an outstanding artist and jewelry designer to boot. He was raised near Ennis and learned to fish in these waters.

# Chapter 23

# Nevada

Nevada is not all bright lights and slot machines. There are a surprising number of excellent trout opportunities both in lakes and streams. In fact, I have seen a nice brown trout caught on the Truckee River right in the middle of Reno!

*Lou Onesty with his "Christmas" fish at Pyramid Lake.*

## *Pyramid Lake*

The largest subspecie of cutthroat trout, the Lahontan cut-throat, lived in Pyramid Lake. Fish larger than 50 pounds were common until they were slaughtered by the thousands in the early 1900s. The result was their extinction. The Walker Lake Lahontan was reintroduced into Pyramid Lake and has done well. Still listed as a threatened specie, they can be caught on this beautiful, if stark, lake on the Paiute Reservation a little over an hour's drive east of Reno. These Walker Lake cutthroats do not get as big as the original Pyramid Lake variety. Still they are far bigger than most cutthroats and great fun to fool on a fly.

A great fishery, it is open from October to June. Check with the Pyramid Lake Paiute Tribe at 775–574–1000.

This fall, winter and spring fishing is fairly straight forward. Find a likely-looking spot on shore, perhaps at a point, possibly where you see others fishing. Use a 7–weight rod and cast large weighted woolly buggers or streamers from shore. Hang on! These fish are large with 20–inchers not uncommon.

Some fly fishers gain better access to deeper water by using a float tube or a boat. Others resort to a unique alternative…the step ladder. Trust me! They take a ladder out about as deep as they can wade and set it up on the bottom. Then they climb up and start casting. Why? Remember this water is cold so getting out of the water helps keep you warm. Plus, getting up higher allows longer casts. To get the flies down, some use weighted tip sink lines, others use spit-shot. The height makes these cumbersome rigs easier to cast. Dress warm, the cold water can cause hypothermia quickly. Numb feet and shivering means you should get out and warm up.

## *Other Waters*

There are many other waters in Nevada that provide interesting fly fishing. There are numerous large reservoirs, some holding trout, others bass and striped bass. Many high country streams and creeks hold populations of trout both Lohontan cuts and non-natives. Explore. You will be amazed at what you will find.

# *Sources of Information*

## *Guide Books*

Dave Stanley, **Guide to Fly Fishing In Nevada** (David Communications, Sisters, OR).

Richard Dickerson, **Nevada Angler's Guide: Fish Tails in the Sagebrush** (ISBN: 1-57188-100-X).

## *Articles*

Richard Dickerson, *Lohontan Cutthroat Trout: A Fly-Fisher's Winter Challenge*, Flyfishing and Tying Journal, (Winter 2000), p.18.

Jason B. Dunham, *Bringing Back the Lahontan Cutthroat Trout*, Trout, (Spring 1998), p.20.

Ralph Cutter, *Win, Lose or Fish: Reno*, Trout, (Spring 1998), p.31.

Anonymous, *Solving the Jawbidge Jigsaw Puzzle*, Trout, (Winter, 1998), p.46.

Richard Dickerson, *Fly Fishing Nevada's Jawbidge Mountains*, Flyfishing, (Nov/Dec, 1997) p.69.

Chip O'Brien, *Nevada's Knott Creek Reservoir*, Western Fly Fishing, (May–June 1996), p.18.

Richard Dickerson, *The Independence Loop*, Western Fly Fishing, (May–June 1996), p.73.

## *Contacts*

**Reno Fly Shop** 775–825–3474. Helpful sources of information, supplies and guides for Nevada and the neighboring California waters.

**The Gilly**, Sparks, NV 775–358–6113. This shop supplies everything for the fly fisher, the spin caster and the hunter. Lots of friendly advice.

*Chuck Rizuto with a 22–inch rainbow caught sight fishing on
the San Juan River, New Mexico.*

# Chapter 24

# New Mexico

An undiscovered fly fishing dream—well relatively undiscovered anyway—is New Mexico. When one thinks of New Mexico they think of the San Juan below Navaho Dam. True, it is full of large fish, but it is also full of fishers. Fortunately there are lots of other waters in the state to keep one happy.

## Taos/Santa Fe Area

The Taos/Santa Fe area offers numerous fly fishing opportunities in streams and lakes. Some provide fishing all year while a few are frozen over in the winter. Most streams drain into the granddaddy of them all, the Rio Grande.

The Rio Grande comes down from Colorado as a fairly big river. In upper New Mexico it cuts through a deep canyon where access is limited, usually requiring a significant hike in and, more importantly, up and out. However, down in that canyon is reputed to be some of the best trophy browns and rainbows in the west. Figure out how to get to them and you could be in lunker heaven.

From Pilar downriver the canyon opens so access is easy and fishing can be quite good. This area holds browns and rainbows and, a surprise, large northern pike. Pike to 40–inches are caught occasionally on flies in the winter months. Winter fishing is uncrowded and fairly good.

Entering the Rio Grande above Taos is the Red River. Don't let the name fool you. Most of the time it is clear and full of rainbows and browns. During fall spawning runs browns gather at the confluence and run up the Red to spawn. I have never fished there during the fall spawn, but I hear it can be fantastic.

I have often fished downstream from the Red River Hatchery near Questa in the winter and spring. I hike downriver from the parking lot and fish back. This section of the river is open all year. It is also a main access to the Rio Grande but somewhat of a long hike on an unimproved trail. During the rest of the year there are numerous locations upstream of the town of Red River that provide good fishing. By the way, if you go to the hatchery area be sure to look at the big pool at the visitor center to see rare albino rainbows.

*Overlooking the San Juan River from Navaho Dam.*

The Red is only one of many good streams in the area. These streams, which are in high country, fish best in summer and fall. Check the guide books or contact local fly shops.

## San Juan

The San Juan River below Navaho Dam is the most popular water in the west. On a bleak winter day threatening snow there will be 40 or more cars in the parking lot at Texas Hole. Fly fishers will stand shoulder-to-shoulder along the popular runs and they are wandering everywhere. Sounds like an impossible situation in which to catch fish, but it isn't. The fish have adjusted to the situation so that a passing fly fisher, even one who walks through their favorite lie, is taken in stride. They move out of the way of the feet and resume feeding shortly. The trout had to adjust or they would have little time to eat!Most of the fly fishers catch a number of rainbows from 14– to 20–inches each day. Some do much better.

True, these fish have been caught again and again; the beauty of catch-and-release being very evident here. True, they do not fight like most wild trout of the same size. True, they usually take impossibly small flies, emergers of No. 20 to No. 24 being standard fare. But where else will you find so many willing large trout?

The trout in the main runs are usually caught with a nymphing rig. Indeed this is where I learned this technique. (See Chapter 7.) It is also where I caught the two biggest rainbows of my fly fishing career (so far).

The side channels also hold lots of trout. Some are continually taking emergers and are maddingly difficult to fool. Every once in a while I figure out something that works. I am so proud of myself...I finally have the secret. The next day it doesn't work and I am back on the search again! Frustrating, but great fun.

The San Juan fishes well almost every day of the year. The water release is fairly constant as is its temperature. Access is easy. The river can be floated or wade-fished. If you don't mind the somewhat battle-scarred trout and crowded conditions, it is a great place.

There are lots of other locations in New Mexico. The Chama area has several guest ranches with pond and/or river fishing. There is public river fishing here too. Around Albuquerque there are several nice streams to fish all year. Further south Elephant Butte Lake has good stripped bass and black bass fishing with trout fishing in the Rio Grand tailwater below it. As with other states, it is amazing what you can find when you explore. Check out the Gila River in the south for beautiful scenery, a great cliff dwelling and good trout fishing.

## Sources of Information

### Guide Books
Rex Johnson Jr. and Ron Smorynski, *Fly-Fishing in Southern New Mexico* (University of New Mexico Press, 1998).

Craig Martin (Ed) *Fly-Fishing in Northern New Mexico* (University of New Mexico Press, 1991).

Ti Piper, *Fishing in New Mexico* (University of New Mexico Press, 1989)

## Articles

Taylor Streit, *Remembering The Red River,* Fly Rod & Reel, (Sept/Oct, 2000) p.8.

Bill Dyroff, "Fishing," *Outdoors New Mexico*, (1999), p.20.

Doc Thompson, *Rio Penasco,* Fly Fish America: Rocky Mountain Edition, (May, 1999) p.20.

Michael Norte, *One Last Time Before The Lights Go Out, Gila Trout,* Flyfishing, (May–June, 1998), p.48.

Michael Kimmel *Taylor Strait, My Grandfathers and Some Pretty Little Fish,* Fly Rod & Reel, (July/August, 1998), p.46.

Hartt Wixom, *Secrets of the San Juan,* American Angler, (July/Aug, 1998) p.46.

Ron Reif, *San Juan River,* Flyfishing (Jan-Feb, 1998) p.52.

Wes R. Smalling, *Red River,* Fly Fish America: Rocky Mountain Edition, (1998) p.18.

Jack Samson, *Rio Grande: Unlikely River of Large Trout,* Western Fly Fishing, (Jan–Feb, 1997), p.6.

Steve Larese, *Fly Fishing in the Land of Enchantment,* American Angler, (Sept/Oct. 1996), p.42.

## Contacts

*The Reel Life Fly Shop* 505–995–8114, 505–268–1693. Located in Albuquerque and Santa Fe, these folks really know about New Mexico fly fishing. Call for guides or information.

*The Timbers* (Fishing Lodge), Chama 505–588–7950. A beautiful lodge on a working ranch with numerous trout ponds and streams. One cabin is next to a pond where I couldn't keep my fly out of a trout's mouth. The stream right next to it is good fishing too.

*Rizuto's San Juan River Lodge* 505–632–1411. (See Abe's below.)

*Abe's Motel & Fly Shop* 505–632–2194…Across the street from one another, Rizuto's and Abe's know the San Juan. Book a guide from them to learn the river quickly. Chuck Rizuto is a great person to learn from if you can catch him between bass tournaments.

# Chapter 25

# Oregon

One does not hear much about fly fishing for trout in Oregon. Makes one think there is not great fishing here…not true! I think they are keeping it a secret from the rest of us. You do hear about the steelhead fishing which is justly famous.

One of the most legendary rivers in the west, the Rogue, flows west to the Pacific. Yes, it still has good steelhead and salmon runs as do numerous other coastal rivers. At a campground on the Columbia River, a fly fisher raved about the trout fishing in eastern Oregon on the Donner and Blitzen River—a real stream I assure you. There is also the Umpqua River, one of the best smallmouth rivers in the country. It seems there are plenty of opportunities.

*The Deschutes River passes through a beautiful valley.*

## *Steelhead and Salmon*

Oregon boasts two types of fly fishers: the addicted steelheader and those not so afflicted. The addicted consider casting all day with a long Spey rod to get two follows and one hookup, but no fish, a good day of steelhead fishing. Never having experienced steelhead fishing, I asked several fly fishers and guides about the experience. The general consensus was that it takes a certain type of person and that most people would prefer catching a number of trout or some great salmon with the same effort. Trout and/or salmon fishing is usually available nearby at the same time of year as the major steelhead runs occur.

Depending on the stream and the time of year, there are runs of all five types of salmon in various coastal waters. (For a discussion of the different types of salmon, see Chapter 17.) Most of these runs are in serious trouble with some closed to fishing some years. Check locally to find out about conditions and timing of various runs. In addition to the coastal waters, there are several tributaries to the Columbia River that drain from Oregon and still have some salmon and steelhead runs. Locations and regulations can be complex, so check it out before you go.

One of my fly fishing friends, Rick Covington, told me he had a great experience fishing the Rogue. The river has a unique steelhead run. In addition to adults many smaller steelheads enter the river each year. These smaller fish are called "half-pounders" even though some can be 18–inches and several pounds. They are numerous and, from what Rick tells me, very willing to take a fly. The famous steelhead fight is there and action is far more frequent. The day can be punctuated by an adult steelhead just to add spice. Sounds like a must that I have put on my wish list for the future.

## *Deschutes River*

The Deschutes River runs north through central Oregon to the Columbia. At its upper reaches it is small but fun to fish. By the time it gets to Bend it is a good size river with salmon and steelhead runs and a unique native rainbow, the Deschutes redside.

My first experience with the Deschutes was in its upper reaches. At a place called Mile Camp I was promised a possible

100-fish-day. The fish would be small but plentiful. The advise was right on. In 1½ hours I caught 18 fish (rainbows and brookies) and missed many more. Unfortunately none were over 6–inches. I could not find the 10–inchers that were claimed, nor could I raise the larger fish reported to be found in the deeper pools. The reason is clear. I had little fish up to my fly all the time. The larger fish couldn't get near me!

Talking to locals, I was told that other places nearby had bigger fish, some well over 18–inches. Each local had his favorite, special spot with the promise of exceptional fishing. Clearly this is a place where some searching is required to find the good spots.

*Deschutes River Redside.*

Moving downstream I floated one of the middle sections of the Deschutes at the Warm Springs Indian Reservation. What a beautiful place. High ridges cradle the river. The banks are lined with cottonwood trees. Birds everywhere. The river is large and fairly swift, composed mostly of riffles and runs. The float alone was worth the trip. The fish were a bonus.

The Deschutes redside is a subspecies of rainbows found only in this drainage. Looking more like a cutthroat than a rainbow, a broad, purplish-red paints its side from the gill plate back to the tail. There are fewer spots and a much less green back. The belly has a mottled orangish look. All in all a very attractive fish that looks nothing like a rainbow even though it is classified as a subspecies.

The rules for floating the Deschutes are different from most western streams. You cannot fish out of the boat. It is just transportation between spots. All fishing is wade fishing. In the heavy current this sometimes presented a challenge. The origin of this wade-only rule is lost in the past as is the explanation for why it is in effect.

Our first stop on this float was a place where the only location to anchor was above the run. We waded down and nymphed the current break. My first cast resulted in a beautiful 14–inch redside. My guide, Jerry Wetherbee (888–230–4665) and I simultaneously said, "not a good sign." Whenever I catch a fish on the first cast I have a slow day. Well in this case I had a slow half-day after a great morning. The morning produced some nice redsides on nymphs and dries and a few whitefish.

The afternoon was spent floating from spot to spot and catching an occasional whitefish or chinook smolt. No more trout, but that was just fine. There is just something special about this place. I was at peace. A day to remember.

## Sources of Information

### Guide Books

John Huber, *Flyfisher's Guide to Oregon* (Wilderness Adventure Press, 1998).

John Shewey, **Oregon Blue-Ribbon Fly Fishing Guide**, (ISBN: 1-57188-133-5).

Dave Hughes, **Deschutes**, (ISBN: 0-936608-91-9).

Raven Wing and Brooke Snavely, **Fishing Central Oregon**, (ISBN: 1-882084-03-9).

George Burdick, **Kalmath River Angling Guide** (ISBN: 0-936608-88-9).

Madelynne Diness Sheehan and Dan Casali, *Fishing in Oregon*, 9th Ed., (ISBN: 0-916473-14-7).

## *Articles*

John Skewey, *Thief Valley Reservoir*, Northwest Fly Fishing, (Spring, 2000) p.12.

Carolyn Z. Shelton, *John Day River Smallmouth Bass*, Northwest Fly Fishing, (Spring, 2000) p.9.

Scott Richmond, *Kalmath Basin, OR*, Northwest Fly Fishing, (Spring, 2000) p.48.

John Shewey, *Callibaetis! (Chopaka Lake)*, Fly Fish America: Pacific Edition, (May, 2000) p.36.

Bernie Taylor, *Big-River Rainbows (Deschutes River)*, American Angler, (May/June, 2000) p.48.

Skip Morris, *Crooked River, OR*, Northwest Fly Fishing, (Summer, 2000), p.67.

Gary Lewis, *Ice Lake: Pack-in for Alpine Brook Trout*, Northwest Fly Fishing, (Summer, 2000) p.8.

Deke Meyer, *Steelheading the Lower Deschutes*, Fly Fisherman, (Sept, 2000) p.28.

Ken Morrish, *Upper Rogue River, OR*, Northwest Fly Fishing, (Fall, 2000) p.30.

Keith Ridler, *Blitzen River*, Northwest Fly Fishing, (Fall, 2000), p.8.

Terry Sheely, *Umpqua River, OR*, Northwest Fly Fishing (Summer, 1999), p.48.

Don Roberts, *Season of Mists*, Flyfishing & Tying Journal, (Fall, 1999), p.30.

Skip Morris, *River of Volcanoes*, American Angler, (Sept/Oct, 1999), p.34.

Don Roberts, *Basalt Bass*, Fly Rod & Reel, (Nov/Dec, 1999), p.35.

Scott Richmond, *Deschutes River Caddis Flies*, Flyfishing, (July–Oct, 1998) p.40.

Deke Meyer, *The Other Umpqua*, Flyfishing, (July–Oct, 1998), p.20.

Bernie Taylor, *Oregon's Trophy Trout*, Fly Fisherman, (Sept, 1998), p.64.

Ann McIntosh, *East of the Rain Forest: Oregon's Deschutes and Metolius Rivers*, Trout, (Autumn, 1998), p.61.

Jim Repine, *Ode to the North Umpqua*, <u>Fly Rod & Reel</u>, (May/June, 1997), p.36.

John Randolph, *John Day River*, <u>Fly Fisherman</u>, (July, 1997) p.68.

Marty Sherman, *Rogue River Late Summer Steelhead*, <u>Flyfishing</u>, (July/Oct, 1997), p.50.

Deke Meyer, *Williamson River Trout*, <u>Flyfishing</u>, (July/Oct, 1997), p.47.

Skip Morris, *The Lesser-Known Rogue River*, <u>Western FlyFishing</u>, (May–June, 1996), p.50.

Deke Meyer, *Cutthroat by the Mall*, <u>Flyfishing</u>, (July/Oct, 1996), p.60.

Scott Richmond, *Deschutes Double Vision*, <u>Flyfishing</u>, (July/Oct, 1996), p.50.

## Contacts

The Hook Fly Shop, 888–230–HOOK. Excellent flies and good advice plus very competent and helpful shop people and guides.

*Chunky browns like this are common in the Green River below*
*Flaming Gorge Reservoir.*

# Chapter 26

# Utah

When one thinks of Utah, visions of red-rock arches and wondrous deep canyons come to mind. For trout fishers, the good news is that in the high country surrounding these scenic wonders is another world; one of beautiful wildflowers, pine and aspen covered mountains and clear rivers and lakes. In that water reside some great trout, many of them as wild as the country they live in.

## The Provo Area

Water cascades over a red-rock ledge plunging hundreds of feet into the Provo River. Called Bridal Veil Falls, it attracts tourists from around the world. Highway 189 follows the Provo upstream from here past Robert Redford's Sundance Resort. Tourists are driving next to one of the premiere brown trout streams in the west.

I have had some great days on the Provo. Most of the year the flows are high, requiring careful fishing in the shoreline pockets to be successful. This is a true *fishing on the edge* river. (See Chapter 9.) There are a lot of fly fishers here in the summer, but they are mostly nymphing the middle runs. You can have those edge fish all to yourself.

I use a dry and dropper rig. Look for rocks that create deep pockets or trees and brush that generate an overhang. A Parachute Adams with a Beadhead Brassie is my starting point. If there is a hatch, change accordingly.

Further east on Highway 40 is Strawberry Reservoir. In July the campground is in the middle of a wonderful wildflower meadow overlooking the water...one of our favorite places to camp. The tailwater of the Strawberry produces some excellent fishing for browns, rainbows and brook trout.

East of Strawberry is the Duchesne River, another undiscovered jewel. Access is limited with some unmarked Indian lands where they love to cite people for trespassing, so make sure you know where you are. On the public lands you will find some great fishing.

Here you will find a great summer day of fishing. Go upstream on Highway 35 to where the river splits. The West Fork holds Bonneville cutthroats, a variety of fine-spotted cuts that just love dry flies. They are not big, but they are plentiful and willing. You could fish this beautiful water in the morning.

The North Fork is in a pleasant open valley. Here you will find rainbows, some stocked and some wild. After a leisurely lunch taking in the scenery, have fun with a dry and dropper on this second branch of the Duchesne. No trophies in these waters, but a very pleasant, uncrowded day.

## The Other Utah

My first fly fishing experience in Utah was many years ago. We were visiting my friend Bill Gensel who was stage manager for the Utah Shakespeare Festival in Cedar City. He had learned of a creek above Cedar City that was supposed to hold some good trout. Off we went to discover Duck Creek. During a lunch-time hatch, I caught over a dozen browns on dries in one deep long run. I would cast to a rising fish, hook and land it, step two feet forward and cast to the next. It was an experience that has lived for years in my head, to be recalled fondly whenever I think of southern Utah. Duck Creek remains alive and well, populated by stocked rainbows with some wild browns and brook trout.

The high country northeast of Zion National Park and running north toward I–70 is dotted with alpine lakes and small streams full of trout. Brook trout over five pounds have been caught in the lakes. The streams can hold rainbows, browns, brooks or cutthroats. The weather is nice with warm summer days and cool mountain nights. The season can extend well into fall. Some water is accessible by car, but many locations require 4-wheel drive or a hike to reach. The effort is worth it, but I do recommend that you do some research before hiking in five miles to a lake that holds no fish!

My friend John Campbell, The Outdoor Source (435–836–2372), took me to Boulder Mountain above Torrey, Utah one early summer day. We reached a clear lake surrounded by aspen, pine and tall ridges after a couple of hours of bouncing over a "road" that looked and felt more like a dry wash. The lake was full of typical-size brookies of 6– to 10–inches. I floated in a tube enjoying the scenery; periodically being interrupted by a fish. It was wonderful. John had told me there were big brookies in the lake so I should have been prepared...but I wasn't. Near shore a cast produced an instant response. The fly disappeared in a large boil. A heavy resistance greeted my set which was hard because I did not expect such a hit. A big fish. It was on the line for a second before it snapped the 5X tippet like it was a cobweb. A trophy 5–pounder? I am sure of it but I will never know.

*Brook trout on. Beaver Dam Reservoir, Boulder Mountain, Utah.*

Below Boulder Mountain, flowing east from Torrey toward Capitol Reef National Park, is the Fremont River. This is prime brown and rainbow water. On the property of The Lodge at Red River Ranch it meanders under red bluffs to form large deep undercut banks. The Lodge is a great place to stay and fish, (800–205–6343). Cast a Woolly Bugger to the bank and strip it back. Hang on. Sixteen–inchers are not uncommon and 20–inchers are caught and released regularly. Watch for hatches too, as this is where I caught my "lunchtime rainbow." (See Chapter 2.)

Upstream there is a public water section called Bicknell Bottoms. This is true spring creek water full of wary trout. I did manage to hook a couple, but not the big ones easily visible sipping midges in this clear shallow water. Here is a challenge equal to the best western spring creeks with fish just as big.

The other Utah is full of opportunities to find your own special place. The little guide book by Dale Hepworth tells about 41 creeks just in the southwestern quarter of the state. Along with the high country lakes, they are enough to keep you busy all summer. Below is what I found while exploring a sampling of them recently.

### Antimony Creek

A dirt road takes you into a beautiful valley with high bluffs and a stream lined with big cottonwoods. Sometimes overgrown, the stream is 10–feet across but quite fishable. It contains small rainbows and browns. At the campground the stream plunges over big rocks into a pool where I was surprised by a nice 14–inch brown.

### Beaver River

Above Beaver, Highway 153 traverses a spectacular canyon to reach a high valley. Wild browns and stocked rainbows are found in the section below the canyon and wild trout in the upper reaches. A very enjoyable place.

### Calf Creek

Nestled in a wonderful red rock canyon is a tiny creek full of small brown trout. Roger Furse and Ron Wilkerson, Outdoor Source instructors, introduced me to this treasure between Boulder and Escalante on Highway 12. Careful wading and accurate casts are needed.

### Chalk Creek

A nice open stream in a beautiful canyon that has pool after pool where the streambed has been renovated. Each pool contains willing rainbows. Nothing big, but lots of fish.

### Clear Creek

Imagine fly fishing under I–70. The stream has runs, riffles and pools containing rainbows and browns. Above Fremont Indian State Park is a canyon and open meadow with more public water where rainbows dominate.

### East Fork Sevier River

This is really two different types of rivers. The lower is a winding meadow stream with undercut banks and deep pools. Like the Fremont, it holds some nice browns. Look for the white signs designating public waters south of Antimony. Woolly Buggers are often the ticket here.

Above Tropic Reservoir the East Fork is in high country adjacent to Bryce Canyon National Park. This picturesque meadow stream is small but still contains a good population of brookies and cutthroats. Some hefty browns are found just upstream from the lake.

### Mammoth Creek

The stream below Highway 89 is on BLM land and holds a good population of brown trout. Pay particular attention to the plunge pool from the culvert under the highway. Above the hatchery are some open areas on the Hatch Ranch that look very fishy. Contact Panquitch Anglers for information.

### Panquitch Creek

The lower canyon has wild browns, some of good size, and the area near the road contains stocked rainbows. The creek can be de-watered, so check with Panquitch Anglers.

### UM Creek

Catch tiger trout (brook/brown cross) in this tiny open stream in a wonderful setting.

## The Green

No discussion of Utah fishing is complete without talking about the Green River below Flaming Gorge Reservoir. Here are miles of access to premiere rainbow and brown trout fishing. Popular to be sure, with many float trips each day and lots of bank fishers and waders. Hike up a mile from Little Hole and the crowd thins. You could have the place all to yourself. It is most popular in the summer, but it fishes well all year. Check at the Flaming Gorge Lodge Fly Shop for information on the fishing, supplies and float trips. Don't miss the mammoth trout mounts in the restaurant that have been caught in the reservoir. I recommend at least one float trip to experience this outstanding fishery.

## Sources of Information

### Guide Books

Dale Hepworth, **Southern Utah's Wild Trout Streams** (Utah Wildlife Resources, No Date.)

Dennis Breer, **Utah's Green River**, (ISBN: 1-57188-111-5.)

Steve Cook, **Utah Fishing Guide**, (Utah Outdoors.com, 1999).

### Articles

Bob Newman, *Falcon's Ledge*, Fly Fish America: Rocky Mountain Edition, (Jan, 2000), p.30.

Kurt Finlayson, *Striking It Rich In Cache Valley*, Fly Fish America: Rocky Mountain Edition, (March, 2000) p.30.

Greg Thomas, *Utah's Provo River*, Fly Fisherman, (September, 1999), p.36.

Larry Tullis, *Floating Utah's Green River*, Fly Fisherman, (Dec, 1999), p.28.

Ann McIntosh, *Salt Lake City: The Provo and the Green*, Trout, (Spring, 1998), p.63.

Justin C. Bond, *Utah's Other Waters*, American Angler, (March/April, 1997), p.68.

Bob Whitaker, *Undiscovered Utah*, Fly Fisherman, (Sept, 1997) p.40.

Jim DeMoux, *Strawberry Has Been Born Again*, American Angler, (Nov/Dec, 1997), p.42.

Bob Whitaker, *Boulder Mountain Bonanza*, Western Fly Fishing, (March/April, 1996), p.6.

Chuck McGuire, *Utah's Green River: And Borderline Perfection*, Western Fly Fishing, (May–June, 1996), p.20.

## Contacts

John Campbell, *The Outdoor Source* (435–836–2372). Camp in the high country of Southern Utah to enjoy some great fishing in spectacular scenery or fish the wonderful Fremont River.

*Flaming Gorge Lodge* (435–889–3773).Comfortable lodge, nice restaurant with huge trout on the wall (caught in the reservoir) and a fly shop full of goodies and people knowledgeable about how the Green is fishing.

Pat Nichols, Guide (435–885–3338). My favorite guide on the Green.

Bobbi Bryant and Vince Salvato, *Panquitch Anglers* (435–676–8950). These folks will tell you all about some of the great streams in southern Utah.

*Guide Jim Shuttleworth with a Yakima River rainbow.*

## Chapter 27

# *Washington*

Washington has a wide variety of great fishing locations for salmon, steelhead and trout in coastal streams as well as interior stream and lakes. From reading the literature on the state's fisheries, it appears that the steelhead is king here. If you are not a steelheader take heart, there are some great trout and salmon locations...often in the same rivers.

When fishing in these combined waters, stream etiquette is different. Most steelheaders work downstream. Determine the direction an angler is working before entering a polite distance above or below them. Keep clear of the water they are working toward.

### *Klickitat River*

Sounds like a river from the heart of Alaska, but it drains from central Washington south to the Columbia. It has runs of steelhead and salmon. Although it was early in the steelhead season (the first of August), I thought I would give it a try. The river was large and somewhat off-color, but I had been warned about that.

The lower river dashes through a deep gorge which the fish have to battle up. Then it opens into a series of large runs and riffles. Upstream it winds through a deep picturesque valley. Great looking water. By the way, in addition to a fishing license you will need a permit to park in the several access sites along the river. Licenses and permits are available at local convenience stores, not at the site, so get them ahead of time.

Since it was very early in the run, I gave the lower section a try. I swung large weighted streamers through the runs, working downstream. No fish. No signs of a fish. After trying several locations without success, I switched techniques. Nymphing with a large Prince on top and a small Beadhead Pheasant Tail below, I still got nothing. This rig was reputed to be deadly on this water for steelhead. Perhaps they had not arrived yet, or perhaps I was fishing for them the wrong way or at the wrong place. Or perhaps the steelhead were doing what they do best...frustrating the angler!

The trouble with unknown rivers is that it takes more than a day to learn where the fish are. I am sure there were lots of fish. What I learned in that one day is that they were not where I thought they would be. Next time I will hire a guide to help me figure it out.

## Tieton River

On our way to Mt. Rainier National Park, we drove along the Naches and then the Tieton rivers. The scenery was great and the rivers inviting. Neither is listed in the guide books but there was a fly fisher at their confluence so I got to wondering. At the forest service campground the host told me there were a lot of fish in the river. After a day of sightseeing, I fished for a couple of hours in the evening.

What beautiful water. Crystal clear, it cascaded over and around boulders, through nice runs and into deep holes. Perfect structure for a trout stream. Full of trout it was. They were not big, but in two hours I caught 11 rainbows and cutthroats to 12–inches on a Royal Trude.

The next morning I tried another spot downstream. Again the structure was beautiful, and so was the caddis hatch. I got 9 rainbows in 2½ hours on an Elkhair Caddis and a Sparkle Pupa. The biggest was 12–inches but it did not matter. They were an unexpected treat. In the middle of a hot summer with tourists passing by frequently, this river was not fished. You won't need a guide, the river is easy to read and it is all on public land. Perhaps there are better places nearby, but I sure enjoyed my time on the Tieton.

## Yakima River

The one river in Washington listed by Trout Unlimited as one of the 100 best trout streams in the country, the Yakima, is broad and fast. I fished the canyon section with Jim Suttleworth on a very hot, sunny summer day. We shared the river with tubers, mostly from the local college, cooling off in the water. Not the ideal conditions to catch fish.

The basic technique for fishing this time of year was to float near shore and cast a hopper and dropper nymph to shoreline structure. Undercut grass banks, overhanging trees and occasional boulders created great structure for the fish. Unfortunately the weather was against us. I saw several large fish rise to the hopper but not take it. It was as if they were saying it was too much effort in all this heat! I did get several fish with this technique, one a nice 15–inch rainbow stationed under a great overhanging tree next to a nice pool. I am sure that a couple of cool days would have turn the fishing on.

At regular intervals there were islands and bars which created some slower water on their inside edges. Jim set me up to fish the first of these and introduced me to the wet fly swing. (See Chapter 7). I had hit after hit from small fish and hooked a couple. Jim also introduced me to the figure eight cast. Similar to a roll cast, it is used by Spey rodders to get a lot of line out without the use of a backcast into shoreline trees and grass. I never perfected it, but when I got it close to right it sure moved the line.

The State biologists have initiated an aggressive program to reintroduce salmon to the Yakima. Currently thousands of chinook smolt are being released into the river each year. In the upper stretches they are so thick that you cannot get a fly past them to the trout. I am concerned that the trout may be impacted by this new competition for food. But in the long run successful salmon runs can add significant nutrients to the water and make it even more productive for both trout and salmon. It could make a good river spectacular. Let's hope so.

I did not get any big fish that day on the Yakima, but they are there. Between the Tieton, the Naches and the Yakima there is a lot of great fishing in central Washington.

## *Sources of Information*

### *Guide Books*
Greg Thomas, *Flyfisher's Guide to Washington* (Wilderness Adventure Press, 1999).

Nathan Caproni, *Washington's Best Lake Fly Fishing* (ISBN: 1-57188-027-5)

Stan Jones, *Washington State Fishing Guide: 7ᵗʰ Edition* (ISBN: 0-939936-04-6)

Doug Rose, *Fly Fishing the Olympic Peninsula* (ISBN: 1-57188-099-2)

John Shewey, *Washington Blue-Ribbon Fly Fishing Guide* (ISBN: 1-57188-134-4)

## Articles

Steve Probasco, *Yakama River's Golden Stonefly Hatch,* Northwest Fly Fishing, (Spring, 2000), p.11.

Bruce Holt, *Blackstone Lake,* Fly Fisherman, (July, 2000), p.57.

Doug Rose, *Olympic Mountain Trout,* Northwest Fly Fishing, (Summer, 2000) p.11.

Joe Warren, *Columbia River, WA,* Northwest Fly Fishing, (Summer, 2000) p.42.

John Shewey, *Seep Lakes, WA,* Northwest Fly Fishing, (Fall, 2000), p.52.

Skip Morris, *Anderson Lake, Western Washington's Potential Gem,* Flyfishing, (May–June, 1998) p.8.

Robert Lyon, *Yakima,* Fly Rod & Reel, (May/June, 1998), p.36.

John Shewey, *Rocky Fort Creek, Washington,* Western Fly Fishing, (March/April, 1997), p.58.

Adem Tepedelen, *Washington's Snoqualmie River,* Trout, (Summer, 1997), p.53.

Jim & Carolyn Z. Shelton, *Quiet Season on the Yakima River,* Western Fly Fishing, (July/Oct, 1996), p.6.

John Shewey, *Chopaka Lake,* Western Fly Fishing, (Nov/Dec, 1996) p.76.

## Contacts

**Jim Suttleworth**, Guide, (888–487–4500). Jim guides on the Yakima and on various coastal rivers which offer steelhead and salmon fishing. He also takes parties down to Baja for spectacular saltwater fly fishing.

# Chapter 28

# Wyoming

As you enter Wyoming you are greeted with a highway sign: "High Winds Possible Next 5 Miles." It might just as well say, "Next State." Most of Wyoming is very open and the wind blows long and strong. A fly fisher learns to deal with it. Since this state has some outstanding fishing, it is well worth it! Native cuts, monster browns and rainbows, small creeks, large rivers, alpine lakes and tailwaters; this state has it all. A few places are heavily fished but much of the state is relatively untouched. It's not from lack of quality fishing. Wyoming is one of the least densely populated states in the country so local pressure is low. Traveling fly fishers mostly go past it to Montana. The fish are there, but often not the fishers, at least not in the high densities found in Yellowstone National Park and the nearby Montana streams.

*Snake River cutthroat.*

## *The Snake River Basin*

The sun had dipped behind the western ridge but still illuminated the bluff in front of me. Golden aspen leaves, made even more golden by the setting autumn sun, mixed with vibrant green pines. I cast my nymphing rig upstream and watched the indicator. Just as it twitched I was distracted by a flock of sandhill cranes raucously making their way up river. I got the fish anyway, probably the 10th I had caught in that run so far and I was only halfway through it. I was on the Snake in October and had it all to myself. The trout was a Snake River cutthroat, the native fish of this area. With a distinctive slash, fine spots, silver sides with a blush of orange toward the belly, it was an attractive fish. This wild native wonder is unpolluted by interbreeding with rainbows as they have never been stocked here.

The Snake and its tributaries in Wyoming are a great place to catch native cuts. The river starts in Yellowstone National Park, heads south to the Tetons then through Jackson, and finally west to Palisades Reservoir in Idaho to become the South Fork. Almost its whole length in Wyoming is public water and most is fishable. In the summer you may have to contend with rafters in some sections, but there is enough water to avoid them. The Snake can be fished from shore or drifted.

I have had some wonderful days fishing this area. One day below the dam at Jackson Lake in Teton National Park I was drifting nymphs and catching 14- to 16-inch cuts when I was disturbed by a splash downriver. Over my shoulder I could see a bull moose, antlers still covered in velvet, making his way ponderously across the river.

Another day the 2PM blue-wing olive hatch was greeted by hordes of cuts. Mixed with them were equal numbers of whitefish, some of substantial size. It was the first time I had caught a whitefish on a dry. I never would have thought it possible, but they somehow managed to get that fly into their tiny underset mouth.

Just above Jackson, going toward Teton National Park, is the National Elk Refuge. In it is a nice little stream, Flat Creek. This stream has been renovated by the local Trout Unlimited chapter and is open to fishing spring through fall when there are no elk in the Refuge. It is a meadow stream with numerous bends and deep undercut banks.

One day I arrived just in time for a mayfly hatch. At one run they were up everywhere. Once I found the right fly, I caught several Snake River cuts. There were no mayflies or trout rising upstream or downstream from this one little run. I have never seen such a localized hatch before…or since. Still, I was thankful since it yielded several nice fish in the 12– to 16–inch range.

Downstream from Jackson at Hoback Junction the Hoback River joins the Snake. This August I drove up the river on Highway 191 for many miles without seeing a single angler. Undiscovered can best describe this river. There are some great camp sites on the river as well as numerous pullouts to park in. The river is full of cutthroats that are fun to catch. Why there were no fly fishers here when Yellowstone National Park, a couple of hours north, was jammed with them is a mystery to me.

*Lamar River in Yellowstone National Park offers great fall fishing.*

## Yellowstone National Park

I have had some great days and some poor ones fishing in Yellowstone. Most rave about the Yellowstone River in the Park. My experiences have been only fair some days and very poor on others. I am sure it can be great, but I haven't hit it yet.

On the other hand, I did hit the Lamar River on a perfect fall week. The Lamar valley is most famous nowadays as the site of the first wolf reintroduction in the Park. I fished at several locations on the Lamar east of Tower Junction and on Soda Butte Creek, one of its tributaries. Once I figured out that these fish were holding in the riffles, I did very well. The average fish was 10–inches but I got several in the 16–inch range.

The Yellowstone cut, which these were, is closely related to the Snake River fine-spotted cut, all part of an original Bonneville subspecie. They appear identical. Only the drainage is different. The Lamar joins the Yellowstone and eventually the Missouri River. The Snake is on the other side of the Continental Divide and joins the Columbia.

There is one spot I remember fondly on the Lamar. The river runs through a big open valley. At most points the road is a quarter mile away so you park and walk across the meadow. That day the hike took a bit longer because I have to give a wide berth to a bull buffalo, not an animal you want to confront, especially during mating season!

It was worth it. A nice riffle broke over a shallow shelf into a deep pool. The trout lay just below the break and were feeding. They may have sensed the need to bulk up for winter for they were hitting everything. I stood in one spot and caught fish after fish. Moving a couple of feet across river I caught some more. As I fished I took in the scenery and looked for wolves. I never spotted one but I think I heard one yap. Wishful thinking, perhaps.

I am in the minority here, but my feeling is the Yellowstone National Park is not the place to fish in the peak tourist season. There are lots of great places to fish nearby in Wyoming, Montana and Idaho. Why put up with the crowds on the roads and in the rivers? As for the fall, that's another matter.

## North Platte Drainage

Running north from Colorado, the North Platte has some of the best fishing in the west. The Wyoming portion of the North Platte starts above Riverside where there are several good public access points. The one at Bennett's Peak produced the roundest rainbow I have ever caught. I joke that it was 16–inches long and 16–inches in girth!

At Riverside the Encampment River joins it. The Encampment is itself a wonderful little river. One day on the upper Encampment I caught 5 great browns; each about 16–inches, on drys and from the same small pool. However, most days I catch significantly smaller fish there.

From Riverside the North Platte gains water as it continues north through Saratoga. The most common and usually most efficient way to fish this area is with a drift boat. The high water of spring usually presents a problem for drift fishing on most waters, but if the North Platte is relatively clear, the high water of June is the best time of year to fish it. Some of the upper stretches that are pure wade fishing in August have great drift fishing in June. It is not uncommon to have nymphing, dry fly action, and fishing with attractors to the edge all in the same day.

The fish in this upper region are a mixed bag of rainbows, browns and some fine spotted cutthroats. There is a full range of sizes with 16–inchers being fairly common and much larger fish caught each year. On two different occasions I have caught 18–inch cutthroats here…as large a cut as typically caught in this area.

Below Rawlins (north) the river is impounded by several successive dams. Between two of these dams is a stretch called the Miracle Mile. Really between 6 and 15 miles long, depending upon the height of the water in the lower reservoir, it is home to some great tailwater fishing. Large fish reside there full time and some real monsters come up from Pathfinder Reservoir in spring (rainbows and cuts) and fall (browns).

The Mile…as everybody calls it…is in the middle of nowhere. There is one place to stay that has simple but clean cabins (Miracle Mile Ranch 307–325–6710), no restaurants, limited shopping at the Ranch, and dry camping only. The nearest motel is over 40 miles away on mostly dirt roads. Yet so popular is the fishing here that you find a car or more in every parking area. Don't be discouraged, even when it is crowded there are plenty of places to fish.

I remember several days fondly. I nymphed a deep run in early March. Once I put on enough weight to get down, I caught several nice rainbows and two identical 18–inch cutthroats. On another day two fly fishers were just quitting a nice run. I asked them how they had done. Nothing! What had they fished? Nymphs. There were blue wing olives everywhere but no fish rising. I decided to give a dry and emerger a try. To their amazement and mine, I caught several nice fish on the dry as these unsuccessful fishers stood and watched. You have to be ready for anything at the Mile.

Below Pathfinder and Alcova Reservoirs is another tailwater, Gray Reef. Just becoming known, this section of the North Platte holds some of the toughest fighting fish I have encountered. Large 18–inch rainbows smash a nymph, make lightning runs and many jump numerous times. It is a treat. I had one literally hit the boat on a jump, tangle my line and break it off before I could stop gasping at my surprise. Four of us drift-fished Gray Reef for two hot days in August, each catching several fish to 20–inches with my Australian friend, Richard Osmond, topping us all with a 22–incher.

Wyoming is a great place to fish, one I have plans to visit again and again. The Wind River Range in the center of the state, the area around Buffalo in the northeast, and the many smaller streams in the west remain for me to explore. Perhaps I will see you there.

## Sources of Information

### Guide Books

Ken Retallic, *Flyfisher's Guide to Wyoming* (Wilderness Adventures Press, 1998).

Richard Parks, *Fishing Yellowstone National Park* (Falcon Publishing, 1998).

Robert E. Charlton, *Yellowstone Fishing Guide* (Lost River Press, 1995).

John Baughman, *Wyoming Fishing* (Wyoming Fishing, 1993).

Chuck Fothergill and Bob Sterling, *The Wyoming Angling Guide* (Stream Stalker Press, 1993).

## Articles

Smith Coleman, *Finding The Green River*, Fly Fish America: Rocky Mountain Edition, (Jan, 2000) p.24.

Larry Tullis, *Yellowstone's Slough Creek*, Northwest Fly Fishing, (Spring, 2000) p.8.

John Randolph, *Monster Lake*, Fly Fisherman, (July, 2000) p.54.

Matthew Handy, *Wyoming's Yellowstone Lake*, Trout, (Summer, 2000) p.42.

Larry Tullis, *The Sally Hatch (Green River)*, Flyfishing & Tying Journal, (Summer, 2000), p.46.

Tim Mead, *High-Plains Surprise*, American Angler, (July/Aug, 2000) p.45.

Smith Coleman, *Trout, Bears & Going Home*, Fly Fish America: Rocky Mountain Edition, (June, 2000) p.27.

Craig Thomas, *Green River, WY*, Northwest Fly Fishing, (Fall, 2000) p.44.

Keith Ridler, *Bechler River, WY*, Northwest Fly Fishing, (Fall, 2000), p.12.

John Shewey, *Wind River Range, WY*, Northwest Fly Fishing, (Fall, 1999), p.34.

Craig Mathews, *Yellowstone's Underfished Waters*, Fly Fisherman, (July, 1997), p.72.

John Holt, *Wind River Gold*," Western Fly Fishing (March/April, 1996) p.16.

## Contacts

***Medicine Bow Drifters*** (N. Platte) (307–326–8002). They will take you anywhere from the upper Encampment to Gray Reef.

***Miracle Mile Ranch*** (307–325–6710). Clean, simple cabins with flush toilets and showers in a separate building. Bring your own food to cook, there is no restaurant for 40 miles.

# Chapter 29

## Canada

Western Canada is full of fly fishing opportunities. From coastal runs of salmon and steelhead in British Columbia to classic trout streams in Alberta to wonderful pike fishing in Saskatchewan to true wilderness experiences from the Yukon south...the choices are mind boggling. I don't pretend to know much about it. To learn would take a lifetime, but from what I know so far, it would be a lifetime well spent.

### Kamloops Rainbows

I floated across a small lake trailing a black Marabou Leach. Suddenly the line tightened. I set the hook and the fish took off toward the other end of the lake. Within feet of the wrong end of my backing, the fish jumped. It then headed back to me at full throttle. As I scrambled to reel in line, it jumped near the boat and took off again. Just as I thought I might have lost it, the line tightened again and started screaming off the reel. Another jump, this time with only a little backing out. Finally several jumps and runs later I netted a gleaming 24–incher!

The fish was a Kamloops rainbow, probably the jumpingest variety of trout I have ever caught. I claim that they are half trout/half tarpon. They reside in central British Columbia, making their homes in lakes and streams. They are wild, even the small ones jumping numerous times. It's wonderful.

I was introduced to these great fish in the lakes around Kamloops and Vernon, B.C. There are many high country lakes one can drive up to and fish by float tube or in some cases rental boat. For a real treat, try Douglas Lake Ranch (800–663–4838). The ranch manages several small lakes on their huge property as catch-and-release fly fisheries for wild Kamloops. It is an experience I am looking forward to enjoying again.

This brings us to an interesting question. If these rainbows are such great fighters, why are they not stocked everywhere? The answer is that it has been tried many times. For some unexplained reason, they do not survive well outside their normal range. To experience the true Kamloops, you have to travel to their native range. It's okay, you needed an excuse anyway. You won't be sorry you made the trip.

## Grayling

In the corner of the world where British Columbia, the Yukon and Alaska meet above Skagway, a river empties one lake and enters another. I have no idea what its name is, it is just one of so many. The inlet to the lower lake fans out and creates a wide shelf with a break into deeper water. It looked terribly inviting. The Canadian customs agent at the BC/Alaska border on the way up from Skagway had suggested the spot as a place to catch grayling.

Grayling are noted for their large sail-like dorsal fin, their beautiful iridescent blue sides, and their willingness to take a dry fly. I tied on a No. 12 Black Gnat and floated it on the current. As the fly reached the break into deeper water it was grabbed. A nice 14-inch grayling came to net. It proved to be one of many, many fish that day. I have no idea how many fish there were at that break, but it was lots.

That was a special place. Scenic beauty, a wilderness atmosphere and easy access by road combined with lots of fish made it so. There are uncounted other places just as special waiting for you to discover them. Some are wilderness locations reached only by plane, others you can drive up to.

(For a discussion of pike fishing in Saskatchewan, see Chapter 14.)

## Sources of Information

### Guide Books
Chris Hanks, **Fly Fishing in the Northwest Territories of Canada** (ISBN: 1-57188-080-1).

John Fennelly, **Steelhead Paradise** (ISBN: 0-936608-87-0).

### Articles
Ken Marsh, *Cowichan River Days (Vancouver Isles)*, <u>Fly Rod & Reel</u>, (March/April, 2000), p.44.

*Dick Schultz (left) and guide Kenny Chen with a 46–inch pike from Minor Bay Lodge, Wolliston Lake, Saskatchewan.*

Phil Rowley, *A Stillwater Quartet, B.C.,* <u>Northwest Fly Fishing</u>, (Spring, 2000), p.40.

Steve Probasco, *Blackford Lake, NWT,* <u>Northwest Fly Fishing</u>, (Spring, 2000), p.10.

Dave Vedder, *Canada's Skagit River,* <u>Northwest Fly Fishing</u>, (Summer, 2000), p.6.

Roger Brunt, *Thompson River, B.C.,* <u>Northwest Fly Fishing</u>, (Summer, 2000), p.15.

Jennifer Larson, *Inconnu Lodge, Yukon,* <u>Northwest Fly Fishing</u>, (Summer, 2000), p.13.

Roger Brunt, *Squarmish River, B.C.,* <u>Northwest Fly Fishing</u>, (Fall, 2000), p.13.

Ed Lawrence, *Spruce Lake, B.C.,* <u>Northwest Fly Fishing</u>, (Fall, 2000), p.60.

Roger Brunt, *Cowichan River, B.C.,* <u>Northwest Fly Fishing</u>, (Fall, 2000, p.8.

Duane Radford, *Alberta's Rocky Mountain Cirque Lakes*, <u>Flyfishing & Tying Journal</u>, (Summer, 1999), p.50.

Larry Tullis, *Fortress Lake, B.C.*, <u>Northwest Fly Fishing</u>, (Summer, 1999), p.54.

Lani Waller, *Babine River, B.C.*, <u>Northwest Fly Fishing</u>, (Fall, 1999), p.50.

Philip Rowley, *Stillwaters British Columbia*, <u>Fly Fishing</u>, (March–April, 1998), p.34.

Jim McLennan, *Alberta Trout Preserve*, <u>Fly Fisherman</u> (July, 1998), p.24.

David Lambroughton, *British Columbia: The Last Frontier*, <u>Fly Fisherman</u>, (May, 1997), p.78.

Ian Forbes, *Island Tour*, <u>Western Fly Fishing</u>, (March/April, 1996), p.42.

Chris Hanks, *Two Faces of the MacKenzie River*, <u>Western Fly Fishing</u>, (March/April, 1996), p.25.

Barry Thornton, *British Columbia's High Country Lakes*, <u>Western Fly Fishing</u>, (May/June, 1996), p.6.

Marty Sherman, *Calypso Blossom Time*, <u>Western Fly Fishing</u>, (July/ Oct, 1996), p.30.

## Contacts

***Douglas Lake Ranch*** (800–663–4838). A lodge and cabins if you need them. Camping too. A number of lakes full of Kamloops trout. Great fun on the largest cattle ranch in British Columbia.

***Minor Bay Lodge & Outposts*** (204–982–9680). Trophy pike fishing on Wollaston Lake in upper Saskatchewan. The people are great and eager to please. So are the pike.

# Chapter 30

## *Treat Yourself*

Well, there you have it. My perception on how to fish western waters. You are now prepared to go forth and experience this truly wonderful fly fishing for yourself. So grab your 5–weight and fly box. Let's go.

Remember to enjoy the full experience. Western fly fishing is not about big fish or lots of fish. It is about being in nature and becoming one with it. It is sighting your first wild mink. Watching an eagle catch more trout than you do. Listening for the far off yip of a coyote. Wondering at the beauty of a native cutthroat or rainbow caught in the waters its ancestors lived in before man arrived.

It is also about the fishing. Hanging on for dear life as a king salmon takes you where *she* wants to go. It is watching as trout sip midges in gin-clear water. It is walking a little while and finding yourself in a place that may not have been fished yet this year.

You will be tested by wary trout. Awed by natural beauty. And overwhelmed by the sheer expanse of the west.

It is a special place. Come, enjoy it.